Leadership for Quality in Early Years and Playwork

Supporting your team to achieve better outcomes for children and families

Debbie Garvey and Andrea Lancaster

NCB's vision is a society in which all children and young people are valued and their rights are respected.

By advancing the well-being of all children and young people across every aspect of their lives, NCB aims to:

- reduce inequalities in childhood
- ensure children and young people have a strong voice in all matters that affect their lives
- promote positive images of children and young people
- enhance the health and well-being of all children and young people
- encourage positive and supportive family, and other environments.

NCB has adopted and works within the UN Convention on the Rights of the Child.

Published by NCB

NCB, 8 Wakley Street, London EC1V 7QE
Tel: 0207 843 6000
Website: www.ncb.org.uk
Registered charity number: 258825

NCB works in partnership with Children in Scotland (www.childreninscotland.org.uk) and Children in Wales (www.childreninwales.org.uk).

© NCB 2010

ISBN: 978-1-905818-50-1

British Library Cataloguing in Publication Data

A catalogue record for this book is available from the British Library

The views expressed in this book are those of the authors and not necessarily those of NCB.

Typeset by Saxon Graphics Ltd, Derby
Printed and bound in Great Britain by Hobbs, Southampton

Printed on paper made from sustainable resources

FSC
Mixed Sources
Product group from well-managed forests and other controlled sources
Cert no. SA-COC-001530
www.fsc.org
© 1996 Forest Stewardship Council

Contents

About the authors

Debbie Garvey

Debbie's background includes practitioner roles in the maintained, voluntary and private sectors, as well as facilitating, developing and delivering training, parent support, setting up new childcare and developing a children's information service. She was one of the original writers of the Leeds Quality Assurance framework. Debbie is also an active trainer, writer and speaker on the subject of leadership, mentoring, team building and reflective practice, and the roles these play in quality improvement for the early years education, childcare and playwork sectors. Debbie is an active and enthusiastic supporter of the quality improvement agenda and has facilitated many workshops and training events and spoken on the subject at several conferences. Debbie regularly contributes work to various publications in the field. Debbie was a founder member of, and continues to be an active member of, the National Quality Improvement Network (NQIN), which is managed by the National Children's Bureau (NCB). In January 2007, Debbie set up Stonegate Training Consultancies to advocate quality provision for children, young people and families, alongside quality training experiences for the dedicated practitioners who work with them.

Andrea Lancaster

Andrea is an Early Years Foundation Stage (EYFS) consultant for Sheffield City Council. Her role focuses on supporting and developing leadership and management within the private, voluntary and independent early years education and childcare sector. Early in her career she was a teacher and then a museum educator. For six years Andrea owned and led a successful nursery and out of school business. Like many other people in the sector, when she started managing the nursery, she had no previous experience of leadership and management and there was very little appropriate training available. Through her own studies on quality assurance and quality improvement, Andrea became very interested in the role that leadership played in the provision of high-quality services. Over the last few years her interest has been drawn to chaos theory and complexity science and what they can tell us about organisational change.

Jonathan Wainwright

Jonathan is a senior lecturer in educational leadership and management at Sheffield Hallam University. He has a background in both business and education and now has a particular interest in leadership in early years services. He has worked on the Yorkshire and Humber National Professional Qualification in Integrated Centre Leadership (NPQICL) programme, latterly as lead academic tutor. This has allowed him to spend a great deal of constructive time in children's centres, talking with and learning from leaders from a variety of very different backgrounds. His current research focuses on the issues faced by headteachers who have responsibility for children's centres.

Preface

*The best way to become acquainted with a subject –
is to write a book about it.*

(Benjamin Disraeli)

Who is this book for?

This book is for anyone working within early years and playwork who either has a leadership role or who aspires to having one. There are two main areas of leadership within this field: leading an organisation (for example, as part of the management team) or leading practice (for example, as a practitioner with a specific responsibility, such as Early Years Professional, curriculum leader, Special Educational Needs Coordinator, etc.). It is not necessary to be part of the leadership and management team in order to lead – the opportunity to lead practice is there for everyone, whatever their position in a team. The student who brings in a new idea which is then acted on by other team members is, for example, leading practice.

There is an Irish saying that goes:

Praise youth and it will prosper.

Nurturing the enthusiasm of young practitioners who come up with new ideas will help raise their confidence. After all, they are tomorrow's leaders.

This book is for those interested in leadership and in raising quality, such as Early Years Professionals (EYPs) and nursery management; people ranging from room leaders to children centre managers to playleaders. It is also for those people who work in a support and challenge role within the sector: quality improvement mentors, early years teachers, and consultants and development workers.

What is this book about?

This book is about how quality leadership in early years and playwork settings leads to quality practice and quality outcomes for children and families. In terms of leadership for quality, it is about what is done, why it is done and how it is done.

Supporting the development of leadership skills in early years settings forms part of the statutory Early Years Outcomes Duty (DCSF 2008). Research shows that children make better progress in settings where there is strong leadership and relatively little staff turnover (Siraj-Blatchford and Manni 2007) and that improvement is more likely to happen where there is effective leadership (Rodd 2006), where all staff are involved in the improvement process, and particularly where there are distributed forms of leadership (Munton and Mooney 2001).

Why was this book written?

Having worked in the quality improvement sector, we came to appreciate that there is a strong correlation between the quality of leadership and the capacity for settings to improve. This is reflected in research which shows the importance of effective leadership in raising quality as also in the strong emphasis there is now on improving leadership throughout the sector (DfES 2004, Ofsted 2008 and 2009, Martin and others 2009). Our reason for writing this book was the felt lack of useful, straightforward literature describing both leadership issues and strategies for leading teams to improve quality and ultimately improve outcomes for children and families. In addition, as in the quote from Benjamin Disraeli cited above, we also wanted to find out more for ourselves. We found that the more we learned about leadership, the more there was about leadership to learn. In this book, we introduce some of the research, literature and publications available. This book is a tour of leadership, not an assertion of the best or only way to lead. We are delighted that Jonathan Wainwright of Sheffield Hallam University agreed to support us. His introduction, exploring leadership and management, sets the scene beautifully for the rest of the book.

How can the book be used?

Having both been leaders/managers in the childcare sector and having worked in supporting roles, we realise that the last thing you probably need after a long day at work is a complicated read. The aim is for this to be a practical book; one that you can either read from cover to cover or dip into based on particular need. You will be signposted to some academic literature and research. Included also are a range of 'reflection points' designed to offer you time to think (reflect), an opportunity to try ideas (do) and the chance to consider your own practice (review).

The aim is to help you reflect on the many aspects that contribute to your own practice; your experience, understanding, knowledge and skills of being a leader and being led, and to identify from that vast wealth of information the key pieces that are useful to you, in your context. You will be offered practical ideas, books to read, websites to use and the theory to support this, all of which will hopefully help you develop your own personal leadership.

How can this book help you develop your leadership?

One thing the book cannot do is give you all of the answers and, contrary to the claims in some leadership and management books, there is no one right way to lead a team. There are, however, lots of ways of leading that have been very effective in particular situations for certain organisations. We know from experience that leadership strategies that work in one context may not always be transferable and work in another. In our opinion, one of the most challenging areas of leadership is judging which strategies and approaches are best suited to the context or situation in which you find yourself and the ability to respond to changing dynamics. As you read this book and others you need to think about whether the strategies and approaches you read about are relevant and workable in your leadership context at this moment in time. Michael Fullan (2007, p.125) calls this being a 'critical consumer' of ideas:

> In other words, do not be seduced into looking for a silver bullet. Given the urgency of problems, there is great vulnerability in off-the-shelf solutions. But most external solutions have failed. The idea is to be a critical consumer of external ideas, while working from a base of understanding and altering local context. There is no complete answer 'out there'.

Throughout the book you will be asked to reflect, be given the opportunity to explore some leadership theory and be supported to consider how the leader as a *learner, enabler, mentor, champion*, *motivator*, *problem solver* and *developer* can improve practice. These aspects are key to effective leadership for quality. Effective leaders are mindful of the importance of supportive and nurturing relationships where individuals, teams and communities are enabled to come together to debate, challenge, take risks and find solutions in order to raise quality. Therefore, you will need to explore this book, or indeed carry out other research, to define which strategies work best for you at any moment in time.

For example, as a leader, you would need to answer the following questions:

- How do you encourage your teams to leave their comfort zone, take risks and make mistakes in an environment that supports them to *learn*?
- How do you *enable* staff teams and individuals to take ownership and responsibility?
- How is feedback used? Is giving and receiving of feedback used as a way to *mentor* and support individuals and teams?
- How do you create opportunities for your teams to have autonomy to develop and *champion* their own projects?
- How do you use challenge and change to *motivate* people, rather than cause frustration?
- How do you support people to analyse and interpret information, reach agreements and *problem solve* to find their own answers?
- How do you delegate responsibility to *develop* others' skills, knowledge and understanding?
- How does the above support you and your team to engage in continuous quality improvement (CQI)?

No-one can truly understand what it is like to be in another's shoes, but we hope to support leaders in finding their own answers through sharing some of the key theories, discussing some of our experiences and offering the opportunity for personal reflection. Today's challenge is to empower leaders and managers to plan, implement, sustain, review and evaluate their own and their setting's improvements to ensure effective leadership, continuous quality improvement and better outcomes for children, young people and families.

Acknowledgements

Writing this book has taken us on an exploration of the leadership journey. We had an intrepid team who accompanied, supported and encouraged us – but who also offered challenge and feedback, and caused us to reflect. At times we have needed to motivate and mentor each other. The voyage we have undertaken has brought each of us new ideas, skills and knowledge. All of this has enabled us to explore the leadership journey and to write the book we wanted to write. It will influence our future knowledge, practice and thinking – and lead to new journeys in the future. At the heart of our writing is our belief in the practitioners, leaders and managers who strive to improve the quality of the service they offer to children, young people and families. We wanted to champion the people who do the role every single day.

In particular, we would both like to thank:

Sue Owen at NCB for starting this idea in the first instance and for believing we could do it.

Jonathan Wainwright at Sheffield Hallam University for agreeing to write the opening pages which so beautifully set the scene and for ongoing support along the way.

Paula McMahon and Rebecca Mason-Bond at NCB for their patience, understanding and gentle guidance of two novice authors.

Our friends and family for support, advice, guidance, encouragement and feedback along the way, but particularly to:

Brian, Joe and Tom, for putting up with the loss of their wife/mum over many weekends.

Mick, for his unwavering encouragement, support and belief and for never complaining about having to do the housework on 'book writing' weekends.

The teams we have worked with. We learned so much from each and every person and we hope you have gained something from working with us. This also comes as an apology: if we got it wrong some of the time, then we hope we apologised at the time, and if not, then please accept the apology now.

Thanks also to the people who sensitively and enthusiastically read drafts, and re-drafts, and who gave useful feedback, and to the people with whom we discussed ideas along the way. We would particularly like to thank Elaine for her amazing attention to detail, her honest, insightful comments and her continuing support. Unfortunately there is not room to mention everyone, but you know who you are and thank you for influencing our leadership journeys.

And finally, we would like to thank the leaders and managers with whom we have had the pleasure of working, and who gave us insight, inspiration and the confidence to try.

Every effort has been made to locate copyright holders of the illustrations included in this publication in order to obtain their permission to publish them. Any queries relating to permission to publish this content should be referred to the authors via NCB Publications.

Introduction

An exploration of leadership and management
in the early years and playwork sector

Jonathan Wainwright

Back in 1977 Abraham Zaleznik posed the question: 'Managers and leaders: are they different?' Since then, many people have made attempts to answer this question. In this introduction I want to set out some of the key thinking about this idea, but you will need to decide which of the ideas are useful and important for you.

Murray (1975) suggested that management always involves defining purposes and objectives, planning, managing and motivating people, and controlling and measuring results (p. 365). On a recent National Professional Qualification in Integrated Centre Leadership (NPQICL) programme, we asked the participants what they thought. They seemed to support the following idea.

> *When someone is managing me it feels like I am supported as part of a team with clear objectives and structures within which to operate.*
>
> (NPQICL participant 2006)

Much of our thinking about management comes from early work in factories. Frederick Taylor (1856–1915) is often seen as the father of modern management. Taylor's 'scientific management' looked at the idea that people would be most efficient if they worked in the same way as machines and followed the tenet that engineering principles could be applied to them. This efficiency could be increased using a number of these principles:

- Identifying the right way to do things – discovered by scientific observation and experimentation.
- Selecting and training the right person for the job.
- Providing detailed instructions to get the worker to do things in the right way.

- Putting in managers who did not actually do manual work but took responsibility for the maintenance of these principles.

It is only through enforced standardisation of methods, enforced adoption of the best implements and working conditions, and enforced cooperation that this faster work can be assured. And the duty of enforcing the adoption of standards and enforcing this cooperation rests with management alone.

(Wood and Wood 2000, p. 184)

These principles were dominant in thinking about management until society demanded hourly pay rather than pay based upon output. Some would argue that Taylor's principles allowed factory owners to take unfair advantage of workers but Taylor's contribution has been to legitimise the study of management as a profession.

One of the other major influences on defining management came from Henri Fayol (1841–1925). Though writing at the same time as Taylor, his work was not translated into English until the 1930s. Fayol was the originator of the idea that management has five functions – Planning, Organising, Commanding, Coordinating and Controlling (the work, rather than the people). Fayol is perhaps best known for his 14 principles of management of organisations:

Specialisation of labour
  Workers should be specialists in order to encourage continuous improvement in skills and the development of improvements in methods
Authority
  Managers have the right to give orders and the power to exact obedience
Discipline
  Staff should be obedient and respectful of the organisation
Unity of command
  Each employee has one and only one boss
Unity of direction
  A single mind generates a single plan and everyone plays their part in that plan
Subordination of individual interests
  When at work, only work things should be done or thought about

Remuneration
  Employees receive fair payment for services
Centralisation
  Decisions are made from the top
Single line of authority
  There should be a formal chain of command running from the top
  to the bottom of the organisation
Order
  All materials and personnel have a prescribed place, and they must
  remain there
Equity
  Equality of treatment (but not necessarily identical treatment)
Tenure
  A job for life for good workers
Initiative
  Thinking out a plan and doing what it takes to make it happen
Esprit de corps
  Fayol thought that a team spirit would derive from a single, clear
  command structure and that this would provide strength for the
  organisation

These principles also illustrate that times change and that what
worked in a largely industrial society in the 1930s might not work
now. Today's society is not industrial; it is unlikely that the reader of
this, or much of their community, will be working in a factory.
Similarly, we do not generally have the same view of authority,
single agency working or are fortunate enough to have security of
tenure.

It is not surprising that, until relatively recently, most writers on
management were men. If we set this against the fact that most
workers in the early years sector are female (Siraj-Blatchford and
Manni 2007), we need to be cautious because many writers (for
example, Scrivens 2002) suggest that there are differences in
masculine and feminine management styles.

Mary Parker Follet (1868–1933) is perhaps the only really well known
female management writer of the time. She was chairperson of the
Women's Municipal League's Committee on Extended Use of School
Buildings, and in 1911 she helped open the East Boston High School
Social Center. She was also instrumental in the formation of many
other social centres throughout Boston. Follett suggested that
organisations might function better if based on the idea of power

through others rather than power over others. She recognised the holistic nature of community and advocated the principle of power sharing.

It is interesting, then, that Mary Parker Follet is beginning to be recognised as the source of much of our current discussions on collaborative leadership, conflict resolution, empowerment and the value of inclusion and diversity.

Defining management seems reasonably straightforward, and more modern ideas about management do not vary much from the original ideas of Fayol and Taylor.

John West-Burnham (2004), for instance, says that management is about doing things right, following the identified path and being taught by the organisation. John Kotter (1999) suggests that good management brings a degree of order and consistency, starts with planning and budgeting, develops capacity by organising and staffing and achieves by controlling and problem solving.

Leadership is often perceived as a very different animal:

> ... leadership is like the Abominable Snowman, whose footprints are everywhere but who is nowhere to be seen.
>
> (Bennis and Nanus 1997, p. 19)

And a clear definition is elusive. Kellerman and Webster (2001) suggest that studying leadership is a good thing because it forces us to face up to:

> ... some of the most complicated and richly textured questions about the nature of human affairs and allows them to set their own parameters for discussion.
>
> (p. 468)

Some of the earliest work on leadership tried to identify the personal characteristics of effective leaders. These have been put into five groups by Gregoire and Arendt (2004):

Surgency	Traits such as energy, assertiveness and extroversion
Conscientiousness	Traits such as dependability, integrity and the need for achievement
Agreeableness	Traits such as optimism, helpfulness and affiliation
Adjustment	Traits such as emotional stability, self-esteem and self-control
Intelligence	Traits such as inquisitiveness, open mindedness and being learning oriented

We can see echoes of this approach today. Jillian Rodd (2006), for instance, talks about the personal qualities of early childhood leaders, whilst Jones and Pound (2008) offer us a table of characteristics, skills and attitudes.

Psychologists working in the 1950s started to base their thinking on what leaders actually do rather than who they are. Early work identified that behaviour could be divided into the attention paid to the job (task) and the concern paid to relationships (see, for example, Blake and Mouton 1964). Such studies identified that the best leader was one who devoted as much energy to achieving the task as they did to looking after their people.

As you will know from your experience, having certain personal characteristics and being concerned about both the job and the team is only part of it, and what works in one situation might not work in another. This may be the case particularly when working with those from a different professional heritage or background.

Researchers also realised this and one of the first situational approaches was explored by Tannenbaum and Schmidt in 1958. Their work suggested that the appropriate leadership style, in a given situation, depended on the manager, their staff and the context. Tannenbaum and Schmidt were amongst the first to suggest that one style of leadership was not effective in all situations.

Some researchers now think that leadership is more about the interaction between leaders and followers and the emotional components involved in this interaction.

As another children's centre leader put it:

> When someone is leading me it feels like I have a choice and am personally valued. I trust the leader's vision and am comfortable to follow.

These ideas are explored more fully in the rest of this book. However I want to conclude by exploring differences.

What do you expect from leadership – is it different from your expectations of management?

Many writers do suggest a difference: As we saw, Zaleznik (1977) first wrote that managers and leaders were two different types of people. He contended that managers seek order and control and excel at defusing conflicts and ensuring that day-to-day activities are accomplished. Leaders, conversely, thrive on chaos and are continually looking for new opportunities and different ways of achieving goals.

Bass and Stodgill (1990) suggested that:

> Leaders manage and managers lead, but the two activities are not synonymous. Management functions can potentially provide leadership; leadership activities can contribute to managing. Nevertheless, some managers do not lead, and some leaders do not manage.
>
> (p. 383)

> Leadership is different from management, but not for the reasons most people think. It has nothing to do with having charisma or other exotic personality traits. It is not the province of the chosen few. Nor is leadership necessarily better than management or a replacement for it. Both are necessary for success in a complex and volatile business environment.
>
> (Kotter 1999, p. 102)

Tim Simkins (2005) however offers an account of emerging thinking which suggests that trying to make distinctions between leadership and management are unhelpful:

The traditional view	An emerging view
Leadership resides in individuals	Leadership is a property of social systems
Leadership is hierarchically based and linked to office	Leadership can occur anywhere
Leadership occurs when leaders do things to followers	Leadership is a complex process of mutual influence
Leadership is different from, and more important than, management	The leadership/management distinction is unhelpful
Leaders are different	Anyone can be a leader
Leaders make a crucial difference to organisational performance	Leadership is one of many factors that may influence organisational performance
Effective leadership is generalisable	The context of leadership is crucial

The emerging thinking seems to fit rather more with our current models of working in multi-agency organisations within the early years education, childcare and playwork sector.

Let us go back to our early years leader who explains:

When someone is managing me effectively I feel that I have a voice, encouraged and empowered, which makes me feel relaxed about how and why I am doing my role. I also feel encouraged and empowered to take ideas further.

When someone is leading me well I feel as if I share their vision. It can be so rewarding. I feel motivated, valued, inspired and excited.

When someone is managing me ineffectively, I feel disempowered – as if I have to do what I am told, fearful of doing a job wrong, which makes me feel watched, restricted and not in control.

When someone is leading me but I do not share the vision, I feel isolated, disempowered, de-motivated, confused about my role and not confident that I can make a difference.

Maybe there are some differences between leadership and management. Earlier thinking says that there are, but perhaps worrying about these differences may simply act as a distraction from our tasks. Perhaps we need to spend our time thinking about how we can work with and inspire our teams in our particular context so that, through them, we can make a real difference to the lives of our children, families and communities.

1 Developing your Leadership

*You do not lead by hitting people over the head –
that's assault, not leadership.*

(President Dwight D. Eisenhower)

There is much published about being a manager and a leader but
very little set in the context of the roles that many of us have within
early years and playwork. It is hoped that within this chapter, and
throughout the book, as you begin to explore some of the theory,
academic research and published materials that are available, you
will feel enabled to use what is appropriate for your style of
leadership, your role, your team and your personality. In other
words, this book is intended to empower you to become a better
leader, using strategies appropriate to the context of your
leadership.

No one leadership style is right. Nor is the way you lead now the only
possibility for you. You may change your way of leading in a small
way or change it completely. A new situation may require you to
change your way of leading or it may give you the opportunity to try
a new approach.

Describing leadership styles

Many of the management manuals currently available are written
from a single perspective and encourage the reader to believe in the
theory or solutions put forward by the author – promoting it as the
only or preferred way of being. In effect they are saying: 'If you
behave in these ways all of your troubles will be over'. This book
works on the premise that in order to improve your leadership, you
need to be able to evaluate your current practice whilst also

reflecting on the range of leadership options available to you and considering the different contexts within which you are working.

The Introduction has established that ideas about leadership and management have developed and changed over time. Most of us will have experienced different styles of leadership and management in our own lives, for example, in education, in sports teams, within family relationships, within friendships and in our working lives. We will have opinions on what works well, feels comfortable and engages us as followers and what does not. If we were each to describe leadership it is likely that some common themes would emerge, but our descriptions would be influenced by our own experiences and by what is important to us as individuals and within our own cultures. In order to explore leadership it would therefore be useful to have a shared understanding of some of the more commonly used terms that writers use to describe it. This should also be of benefit as you delve further into research on the subject.

Heroic and post-heroic leadership

The terms 'heroic' and 'post-heroic' focus on the characteristics of the leader.

Heroic leadership is a way of describing individualised, charismatic, inspirational leaders. These leaders appear to have all of the answers and they command their followers. Heroic leaders are not necessarily manipulative or 'bad'. Another way of describing this leadership style is that followers are content to be told what to do. If you think back through your life (perhaps school and playground experiences from your childhood), we are sure you will be able to think of good and bad experiences of being led or influenced by a leader using a heroic style.

Post-heroic leadership is the opposite of heroic leadership. It refers to socialised, inclusive and collective leaders. These leaders can also be charismatic. Again, think about the times you have been led or influenced by someone using a post-heroic style. Perhaps you felt you were able to make choices or you felt your voice was heard in a decision making process – even if the resulting decision was not what you wanted.

Transactional and transformational leadership

The terms 'transactional' and 'transformational' focus on how leaders work with their followers.

Transactional leaders tend to focus on getting things done and make use of systems of reward and sanction. They may tend to a more heroic, individualised style of leading. Rewards may have a monetary value such as pay rises, bonuses and awards, whilst sanctions may take the form of a smaller or no pay rise or bonus. Transactional leaders can also use their time and attention as currency in rewards and sanctions. In other words, they might spend time with you when they are pleased with your work but they might show their displeasure by being unavailable and perhaps avoiding you completely.

When identifying this form of leadership in your past experience it would be useful to consider how it made you feel on occasions when you achieved and on occasions when you tried but failed. Would your response be different if you recognised that it was the result, and not you, that the leader cared about?

Transformational leaders are so-called because of the transformation or change that occurs within the follower. This might be in terms of learning and development or could be described as job satisfaction or personal fulfilment.

It is concerned with emotions, values, ethics, standards, and long-term goals and includes assessing followers' motives, satisfying their needs, and treating them as full human beings. Transformational leadership involves an exceptional form of influence that moves followers to accomplish more than what is usually expected of them. It is a process that often incorporates charismatic and visionary leadership.

(Northouse 2007, p. 175)

Distributed and devolved leadership

You may come across references to 'distributive leaders' or 'devolved leadership' where leadership responsibilities are shared. This leadership style usually refers to the disposition or willingness of the leader to share responsibility, rather than the organisational structure dictating that it happens. Trust is often a major factor in the success of this approach as the leader is ultimately accountable for results or outcomes. Think of leaders you have worked with who gave you responsibility to carry out your role and trusted you to do the job.

Laissez-faire leadership

This term is used to describe someone in a leadership position who does not lead but leaves followers to get on with it without involvement, direction or support. This kind of leader can seem almost disinterested in the team and have little day-to-day involvement in what happens. Sometimes this style of leadership occurs because the person is too busy with other things to attend to the team or individuals.

Authentic leadership

Authentic leadership refers to the ethical and moral aspects of leadership. In this, definition traits such as integrity and honesty are key factors. Behaviours such as bullying would belong to an inauthentic leader.

Situational leadership – employing a range of leadership styles

Reading the descriptions of leadership above, you should have recognised that you and other leaders in your experience do not fit neatly into one category. Leaders develop their leadership capabilities and style over time and through experience. They use different styles according to their preferences, ability and the context in which they find themselves. Daniel Goleman and others (2002) identifies six leadership styles: Commanding, Visionary, Affiliative, Democratic, Pacesetting and Coaching.

Goleman argues that the very best and most effective leaders are ones who have mastered at least four of the six styles he has identified and are able to use them flexibly according to the situation. The four styles he believes are most prevalent in effective leaders are: the visionary, democratic, affiliate and coaching styles.

The traits approach to understanding leadership

The traits approach to understanding leadership focuses on the personal qualities and behaviours of the leader. Northouse (2007, p. 33) lists ten leadership traits:

- articulate
- perceptive
- self-confident
- self-assured
- persistent
- determined
- trustworthy
- dependable
- friendly
- outgoing.

Whilst these traits can be seen as essential dispositions and characteristics of an effective leader, for example, being persistent in finding a way to achieve an organisational goal, the approach is limited by the number of traits listed – where, for example, is creativity in finding solutions to problems? This approach looks at the *how* but not the *what* of leadership.

The use of competency frameworks

The competency approach to understanding leadership focuses on the knowledge, skills and understanding required to be a leader. It looks at a person's ability to do the job – at the *what* but not always the *how*. (See also Moyles 2006, who combines a competency approach with a traits approach in her Effective Leadership and Management in the Early Years [ELMS] evaluation tool for early years leaders.) Competency frameworks are increasingly being used to train, develop, appraise and recruit leaders.

A well-known example of a leadership competency framework is the Master of Business Administration (MBA), which is recognised throughout the world as a way of developing leaders and managers for all types of careers. For leaders and managers in the early years sector, there is the Early Years Professional (EYP) programme, the National Vocational Qualifications (NVQs) at Level 4 for leaders and managers and the National Professional Qualification in Integrated Centre Leadership (NPQICL) programme – all of which use competencies and standards.

To be accredited with these qualifications, potential or existing leaders and managers have to prove that they have the required knowledge, skills and understanding. A flaw in this approach is that people are often accepted onto courses without prior experience of being a manager, or in the case of EYP, prior experience of working in the early years field. Discussing MBAs, Mintzberg (2004) argues that these accredited training courses are more appropriate and valuable to existing managers who can reflect on their past experience of leading and managing. Another weakness in the competency approach is that leadership happens in context. A leader may display competency in a particular skill or area of practice in one situation. However, when in a new situation or organisational context, that same skill may not be appropriate or effective. Key leadership skills can be considered (and sometimes taught) in isolation, but effective leaders need to use a judicious combination appropriate to the situation in order to produce the desired results.

📖 Reflection: case study

Leadership image

Trevor is the owner/manager of a large out-of-school club. Even though Trevor has been in this position for four years now and his organisation is successful, his team stable and happy, he says he feels like an impostor. The problem is that he believes he does not live up to his image of a 'manager' and feels uncomfortable when someone describes him as such or, worse still, as a businessman. The image he has of a 'manager' is of someone who can make ruthless decisions, who cares about the bottom line first and foremost and who is a 'success'. He does not quite know where this image comes from but he feels that he falls short. Trevor says he feels like part of the team and often says that he only feels he is responsible for the organisation when he is worried about finances.

- Why do you think Trevor feels the way he does?

- What issues would you ask Trevor to reflect on?

Aspects of the leadership role – the 'what?' and 'how?' of leadership

The earlier section explained the terms used to describe the variety of styles that leaders display and that are generally acknowledged within the leadership and management community. These styles describe how leaders lead. Throughout this book, however, you are encouraged to think about what leaders do (learn, enable, mentor, champion, motivate, problem solve, develop) and put this in the context of how effective leaders do it using their personal attributes (traits) and their skills and knowledge (competencies).

Each aspect of the leadership role is linked and although they are looked at in individual chapters, they should be considered as essential parts of a whole. (Imagine a leader who was only able to champion or only able to problem solve). The best leaders are competent in all aspects of the leadership role, described below. However, it is important to recognise that, dependent on factors such as experience, knowledge, context and personal preference, individual leaders will focus on some aspects more than on others.

The Leader as a Learner
Effective leaders are constantly reflecting on and learning about their practice in a variety of ways. Good leaders create a learning culture where they model and support formal and informal learning opportunities. They foster an emotional environment where teams feel enabled to honestly reflect on their practice, take risks and try out new ideas.

The Leader as an Enabler
Effective leaders support their teams to deliver high-quality services by finding out what helps and what hinders practice. They support practitioners to understand their roles and responsibilities and empower them to self-regulate and to suggest and implement improvements.

The Leader as a Mentor
Effective leaders use techniques and approaches traditionally associated with mentoring (and the associated disciplines), such as developing autonomy, supporting reflection and offering challenge.

The Leader as a Champion

Effective leaders are ambassadors for their organisations. They have a vision that they develop and share with others. They act with integrity and lead by example, standing up for what they believe is right.

The Leader as a Motivator

Effective leaders care for others. They understand the importance of emotionally intelligent relationships and place value on creating positive working environments in which practitioners feel fulfilled.

The Leader as a Problem Solver

The Leader as a Problem Solver knows that prevention is better than cure. The best way to manage problems is to have processes in place to avoid them being created in the first place. When problems do occur, leaders should have a range of strategies to assist them and endeavour to learn from the situation. Leaders should not work in isolation but should develop strong supportive teams that are capable of identifying and solving problems themselves.

The Leader as a Developer

Effective leaders promote an ethos of continuous quality improvement (CQI). They encourage practitioners and other stakeholders to be reflective and to suggest and implement improvements. They enable the sharing of good practice and networking with other organisations.

Describing organisations

... in times of change it is vital to be in touch with assumptions and theories that are guiding our practice and to be able to shape and reshape them for different ends.

(Morgan 1997, p. 376)

Leadership occurs within a context (or situation), for example, a family, a classroom, an army or a nation. Leaders may have a preferred style of leading but will often use a variety of styles and approaches depending on the context and situation. For example, leaders may normally be inclusive and collaborative, sharing responsibility with the team, but in the face of a threat to the organisation may choose to adopt a more authoritarian style and make all of the decisions themselves. You may be able to think of a leader who uses different styles and approaches with different groups of colleagues within their organisation. The context for the leadership discussed in this book is that of the organisation (regardless of size). Each individual setting or organisation represents a different context. What is appropriate or works well in one context may not work well or be appropriate in another.

The way leaders see their organisations also has an impact on how they behave. Morgan (1997) uses a number of metaphors to describe organisations: the organisation as a machine, as an organism, as a brain, a culture, a political system, a psychic prison, as flux and transformation and as an instrument of domination.

Morgan argues that leaders and managers who are able to see the same organisation through a number of these images have an increased chance of solving organisational issues, first, because they are aware of the strengths and weaknesses of each of the ways of thinking about an organisation and, secondly, because having the ability to accept that there are different ways of looking at an issue increases the leader's capacity to innovate and find new ways of working.

The following table gives a brief explanation of Morgan's metaphors for (ways of thinking about) organisations:

Metaphors for ways of thinking about organisations (Morgan 1997)

The organisation as ...	Understanding the metaphor
a machine	People are all interchangeable parts of the organisational machine – cogs within a wheel
an organism	Organisations are living systems that are adapted to their surroundings and some organisations are more suited to some environments than others
a brain	Organisations are intelligent learning systems
a culture	Organisations are systems based on shared beliefs, values, meanings and understandings; the organisation is the enactment of a shared reality
a political system	Organisations are a system of government; conflict of interests, power and control are the focus of this metaphor
a psychic prison	Organisations are manufactured/created by the way people think and act so if we think of an organisation in a particular way, we may be trapped into not being able to think or behave in other, perhaps creative, ways that may ensure the ultimate survival of the organisation
flux and transformation	Organisations are in a constant state of change and transformation so how we seek to understand and perhaps manage the changes depends on the science we use
an instrument of domination	Organisations use and exploit their employees

Looking at the descriptions of the metaphors:

- Is there one metaphor that you feel is more meaningful for you than others?
- Can you use a different metaphor to think of your organisation?
- Do you think other people in your organisation think in the same way or differently to you – what makes you think that?

Your view of the world

Just as the way you see an organisation may affect the way you behave as a leader, the way you see the world may also affect the way you behave as a leader and, in particular, how you approach change.

Your view of the world

How you see the world	The science	View of organisational change
The world is predictable	The world can be explained in a logical, linear fashion. If you do 'a' and 'b' then 'c' will occur. This type of scientific thinking is called Newtonian thinking after Sir Isaac Newton. Things can be understood by breaking them down into smaller component parts. Thus, to understand the human body, you can look at the nervous system, the respiratory system, the circulatory system, and so on.	Machine view of organisations – Taylor's 'scientific management'. Break down jobs into smaller component parts, for example, assembly lines, silos and bureaucracies. The system is designed to be stable but you can introduce and 'manage' changes.
The world is not always predictable	Sometimes unexpected things happen. If you do 'a' and 'b' then 'c' should occur but you cannot always be sure. Albert Einstein was one of the first scientists to challenge Newtonian thinking.	Change can be managed but leaders need to be skilful in managing unexpected changes.
The world is chaotic	Chaos Theory arose from meteorologists using computer simulations to try and predict long-term weather forecasts. Patterns and order were seen to emerge from chaos. Very small changes were observed sometimes to have a huge impact on the system being observed. James Gleick (1987) popularised the science in his book *Chaos: Making a New Science*.	Systems view of organisations. The 'edge of chaos' is seen as a very creative place to be. Change is constant and inevitable. Managers need to be skilful at spotting opportunities that will be beneficial to the organisation.

How you see the world	The science	View of organisational change
The world is complex	Complexity Theory acknowledges that there are periods of stability between the periods of chaos, but also that the stable places are never the same as before. There are many factors that influence change and each situation is different according to the context and the specific combination of influencing factors. Therefore, if you do 'a' and 'b', you cannot expect exactly the same results every time. Margaret Wheatley (1999) writes about complexity in her book *Leadership and the New Science.*	Organisations are complex adaptive systems and are often compared using ecological reference systems. Change is not always constant but can sometimes be desirable. Organisations that are flexible and able to cope with change are more innovative and therefore more likely to survive.

Chapter summary

This chapter begins by discussing commonly used terminology to describe a range of leadership styles. It surmises that leaders often use a mix of or different styles based on preference, ability and context.

The chapter seeks to understand leadership through a range of approaches and frameworks. A traits approach, for example, looks at the personality traits and characteristics of leaders while a competency approach looks at the set of skills and knowledge required of leaders. A situational approach to leadership looks at a combination of the above, namely how leaders apply the skills and knowledge according to their context or situation.

Aspects of the leadership role are touched upon. This is an explanation of not just how leaders lead but what they do. Leadership occurs in the context of (in this case) the organisation. How leaders and others view the organisation has an impact on the way they lead/are led. And finally, the way a person views the world can have an impact on their leadership and how they manage change.

2 The Leader as a Learner

Learning how to learn is life's most important skill.
(Tony Buzan, originator of mind mapping)

The Leader as a Learner

Effective leaders are constantly reflecting on and learning about their practice in a variety of ways. Good leaders create a learning culture where they model and support formal and informal learning opportunities. They foster an emotional environment where teams feel enabled to honestly reflect on their practice, take risks and try out new ideas.

Being a leader is often something that is thrust upon us, and when we take on the mantle of 'manager' within our job titles, we can feel there is an expectation of having to know everything there is to know about being a leader. Similarly there are those of us who have been leaders or managers for many years who still feel as if we are swimming in treacle. This chapter will explore what it means to be a 'Leader as a Learner'. It will look at ways to support the idea that we do not know everything, nor can we be expected to, and how, as leaders, we can support others to see this too. Part of this chapter is about childhood, about how we learn as children and how this influences us as adult learners. It will examine how our preferred learning styles influence our interaction with people, situations and the world around us. The chapter will also begin to investigate how we obtain feedback on our performance and how we use this information to inform future practice.

Rather than looking at recognisable learning experiences, such as training, conferences and workshops, this chapter explores learning on an individual level, and what we as leaders can do to develop learning potential in ourselves and others. Whilst learning from training, conferences and workshops is an important part of learning as a whole, it is what we do with that learning that is important, and that will ultimately improve practice. All of these opportunities – whether formal training, visits to other settings or buddying/ mentoring/coaching arrangements within the setting – cost time and money and therefore need to have an impact. There is no point in accessing these opportunities if no changes to practice are then made possible.

This chapter is about leaders who understand learning, both in themselves and others. There will be opportunity to consider how such a leader not only role models learning and reflection but also encourages a learning culture within the organisation.

The Leader as Learner must lead by example. For example, team meetings should be seen as opportunities to develop learning as well as for sharing information. Reflection should be seen as an integral part of the setting, supporting developments, understanding and the sharing of ideas. Staff should be encouraged and empowered to reflect on their own and others' practice and share feedback appropriately.

Leaders need to ensure that not only are the learning experiences valuable but that they are also valued. Practitioners need to have opportunities to reflect on or discuss what they have learned, try out new ideas, and see how this has a positive impact on practice and ultimately on outcomes for children.

Every situation we find ourselves in has the potential to be a learning environment – if we allow it. We may find ourselves in situations where we think 'This will never work' or 'We have tried this before'. Sometimes it is just the timing that is not right. At other times we think 'There is always room for improvement' and give it our best shot. Circumstances revolve around us, but we are not passive receptors; we have influence on some of those circumstances. It may be that what did not work two months ago will work now.

Just because a person has done something for, say, twenty years does not necessarily make someone good at it. It could simply mean that they have been making the same mistakes for the last twenty years. Or, perhaps, that their practice has stayed the same.

This is where the key early years skill of reflection comes into play: not in terms of reflecting on what the children are doing, but being able to reflect on our own thoughts, words and deeds. How we translate this reflection into practice is one way in which we develop

Gazing into a mirror can be a rather superficial activity. However, the image can be distorted and we may even choose to look at ourselves from a flattering angle. An alternative definition of 'reflect' could be: 'carefully considered thoughts'.

In terms of leadership, the second of these two definitions is more appropriate. To truly reflect on our own practice and make this a meaningful activity involves developing skills of review and analysis, but it also requires attitudes such as honesty and a willingness and determination to devote time to personal improvement. If we are constantly distracted by the pressures of day-to-day work and always put the needs of others before ourselves, if we hardly ever take time for personal reflection, there is a danger that reflection becomes a fleeting glance rather than a critical gaze.

It is also worth thinking about 'reflexivity' at this point. Reflection is now commonly used to discuss how we consider, review and analyse our thoughts and actions. However the term 'reflexivity' is also becoming more widespread.

> *It is useful to define reflection as being careful mental consideration or concentration, and reflexivity as being the ability to direct back on oneself. In the case of professional development, this means directing new learning back into one's professional practice.*

> (www.teachingexpertise.com)

In other words, we can reflect as much as we like, think, consider, review, analyse and so on, but we need to ensure that we use this reflection in a reflexive way, so as to impact on practice.

Reflection and the Leader as a Learner

Moon (2004) discusses the links between learning and reflection:

> *We have essentially defined non-reflective learning as the kind of learning that is unchallenging to the learner ... But is it as simple as this – is this distinction of learning into reflective or non-reflective categories appropriate or are we talking here of a matter of degrees of 'reflectiveness'?*

> (Moon 2004, p. 92)

Can learning happen without reflection? For example, do we reflect when we do the following:

- Learn facts (all of the names of the children in the group)
- Learn by rote without necessarily understanding (learn the eight-times table)
- Learn by copying someone undertaking a task (learn the fire drill)

When we reflect on something, we think about it. Does this thinking allow for the opportunity to review, analyse or be open to other ways of thinking about something? Or is it that there are missed opportunities to challenge our thinking or develop learning? (This does not have to be a total change of opinion; the change might simply be a deeper or broader understanding.)

Similarly, if we are not prepared to engage with reflexivity, and consider how this review, analysis and thinking will influence our future practice, can we truly say that it has influenced our learning?

Moon (2004, p. 92) goes on to say:

> The point made here is that it is not possible to say that a task is reflective or not ... we cannot determine how the internal experiences of another operates.

In other words, how do we know what processes other individuals go through to learn the above? Can we learn a list of names and numbers without reflecting on what they mean to us? Reflection is a skill that can be improved and developed, and can help to improve and develop learning. Using thinking (and reflection) skills such as forming and posing questions, and developing and testing hypotheses, supports the engagement with deep level learning. Moon (2004) discusses how this takes place in relation to the material offered, the structure in which the learning takes place, the depth of the challenge and how the learner shares their learning with others:

> ... reflective learning occurs ... when the new material is challenging.... And the learner wants to understand the material in a manner that is meaningful ... (takes a deep approach).

> (Moon 2004, p. 87)

Developing reflective practice

Reflective practice can enable us to:

- *Study our own decision making processes*

- *Be constructively critical of our relationships with colleagues*

- *Analyse hesitations and skills and knowledge gaps*

- *Face problematic and painful episodes*

- *Identify learning needs*

(Bolton 2001, p. 14)

Is self-reflection a natural skill or can we learn how to do it? What do we do with all those 'carefully considered thoughts' once we have them? Reflection comes easier to some people than others, but is also something we can learn how to do (or even learn how to do better). In her book *A Handbook of Reflection and Experiential Learning*, Jennifer Moon (2004) discusses the following:

> *Since reflection is suggested to be an element in good quality forms of learning, we clearly take the position that everyone can reflect, though this may not always be a conscious activity and may not be done willingly when required…. Assuming that everyone can reflect does not assume that everyone uses reflection effectively to improve performance.*

(Moon 2004, p. 89)

In the way that we all have preferred learning styles, we also have preferred reflection styles. There are a range of ways in which self-reflection can be supported, as outlined below. Which do you engage with on a regular basis?; which would best suit you?; and, are there any that are new to you and that you hadn't contemplated before?

Reflection techniques

Reflective drawing

Some people will prefer to 'draw' their reflections. Much in the way you might doodle, you could begin with a blank piece of paper and draw your thoughts as they come. As long as you know what your squiggles, arrows, dots and lines mean, drawing is a perfectly acceptable way of reflecting. You could begin by creating a drawing in the middle of the page – an image of what the issue is that you wish to reflect on – and then slowly build up the picture as the thoughts come into your mind.

Mind maps

Tony Buzan, whose quote is used at the beginning of this chapter, is generally acknowledged as the person who developed 'mind maps'. This is a useful way of reflecting for visual learners. Some people like diagrams and use space to add extra ideas and thoughts as they occur. Mind mapping is ideal for this. On a blank piece of paper, write in the middle the idea/thought you want to develop, then, like drawing a fat spider's web, draw lines off as thoughts occur, with the idea/thought written at the end of each line. Lines can be linked as ideas develop and new lines can be added as offshoots from original thoughts and ideas.

Free-form writing

On beginning to reflect, some people put pen to paper and write. Even if you are unsure of what to write, it is your reflection; you can write in whatever form you want to: notes, lists, bullet points, poems, recollections of conversations or proverbs. Free-form writing works for some people, especially if your emotions are heavily involved in the situation. It can be a way of getting the feelings whirling around your head down onto paper. This can then often lead to more 'focused' forms of reflection once the emotions are out of the way. That is not to say free-form writing is only useful for emotional reflection; for some people this is their preferred way of reflecting, regardless of the situation.

Unsent letters and emails

Much like free-form writing, unsent letters/emails can be a powerful form of reflection when you cannot sort out your emotions from the situation. Think of all those times you have been angry with a line manager and what you would say if losing your job/professionalism/ kudos did not matter; or the times when you have been frustrated with bureaucracy and red tape. Unsent letters/emails can be useful forms of reflection in these situations. You begin a blank email or letter and write exactly what you are thinking or feeling and what you would like to do if there were no consequences to consider. Then either print a copy (to add to your journal) or delete the letter/ email. This can help separate the emotions from the issues and leave your head clearer to deal with the situation in a rational way. Leave it for a while, then come back later to write the letter/email that it is more appropriate to send.

Unsent letters/emails come with a 'health warning' – make sure you do not put anyone's name in the 'to' line so you cannot send off the email by mistake, and if you do print it, make sure you do not leave it where it may be picked up by someone else. Unsent letters and emails are probably safest done at home.

Talking

As discussed previously, just as we all have preferred learning styles, we also have a preference for a particular type of reflection. For some people writing things down is just not appropriate and they need to talk. We can do this with someone we trust who is willing to discuss the situation over. This can be a verbal form of reflection – as long as we talk to people who we know will ask challenging questions. This is not about 'coffee cup counselling'. It is no good reflecting with someone who will reiterate that things will get better. We need the 'reflective friend' who will say: 'How did that make you feel?' or 'What are you going to do about it?' Very often we feel supported and listened to and come to the conclusion by ourselves. The 'reflective friend' knows this, and much like a mentor, supports us by actively listening and asking the right questions at the right time (see Chapter 4).

Journaling

Journaling is perhaps the most well known written form of reflection and has become increasingly popular over the last few years, particularly in the early years education, childcare and playwork field. Qualifications are increasingly asking for candidates to take up some form of journaling as an expected part of the training. For some the journal is like a portable mirror and goes with them everywhere, for others it is something they have to do for a training course, and for yet others it is a document they add to occasionally when they feel the need. If you have to keep a journal, try not to think of it as a chore. Keeping a journal gives you the opportunity to take some time out and think about your work. You can begin a journal in whatever format you prefer; it could be electronic, within a beautiful book that is kept specifically for that purpose, or within a loose-leaf file that you can add to as you go along. Journaling is similar to free-form writing in that you can write whatever you want. There also are a range of tools to help with journaling and to assist the writer in focusing on particular issues.

> So we are not talking about something with a fixed definition here. The definition [of a journal] has fuzzy edges.
>
> (Moon 2005, p. 2)

Non-paper journaling

Journaling does not have to be on paper. Many people use hand-held tape recorders and verbally record their thoughts. Likewise, electronic journals are becoming increasingly popular and have the added advantage of allowing you to change, alter and adapt as you go along.

In our opinion the best form of reflection is a probably a combination of some or all of the above. However you decide to keep a record of your reflections is ultimately up to you and which system you think works best. It may be that different situations call for different approaches. If you do not know where to start there are some good examples of reflective practice models around. Have a look at the Gibbs reflective cycle (1988), the Johns model (2000) or the model by Rolfe and others (2001), all of which are easily available in books on reflection or on the internet.

Reflection: case study

Journaling

Jo began writing a journal as part of a training course. After the first session, she immediately went and bought a beautiful hardback notebook in which to write down all of her reflections. Within a few days, Jo had filled several pages with reflections on her team, her line management and her emotions.

Later, she was told something that had a bearing on a previous situation. Jo found that because she had already written on the following page, she could not go back to the situation within her journal. Jo stuck a sticky note over the top, and left it at that.

When the situation had been resolved, Jo received a thank you email from her line manager. Jo was delighted with this and wanted to add it to the journal. At this point Jo realised that maybe, as beautiful as the book was, it was not the easiest way to keep a journal. So Jo purchased a bright green A4 lever arch file, photocopied her notes, added the email and sticky note and inserted these into the file. This also means that Jo can add additional pages as required. To make the book appealing, Jo uses stickers whenever she has the opportunity to.

The journal is kept at home where it cannot accidentally be picked up and Jo can write anything, anywhere on any piece of paper and add it to the journal later.

This case study highlights that:

- a journal is personal to you

- you need to be able to add to it as you go along

- you need to leave space to go back and add further comments

- it does not have to be pristine and perfect

- you need to remember to journal good things too

- printed copies of thank you emails/letters are useful to look back on.

Answers to the following questions will enable you to discover the ways in which you might use reflection as an aide to developing learning:

- When will you reflect and what will you reflect on?
- How will you record your reflections? Which reflection technique appeals to you?
- Where can you find more information on reflection techniques?

- Is there someone you can talk to about your reflections?
- Where can you safely store your reflections?

How do we learn?

This chapter has looked in great length at reflection, and although it is a powerful tool for learning, it is obviously not the only way we learn. There is, and has been, much research undertaken into how we learn. Dewey (1953) looked at how we think. Kolb and Fry (1975) looked at learning styles within the model of experiential learning, and the idea that to understand a concept we have to try it out first. More recently there has been much debate about the difference between pedagogy to describe how children learn and androgogy to describe how adults learn, and whether we change our learning patterns as we move into adulthood. It is a generally agreed principle that children learn by making mistakes and trying things out, over and over again if necessary. Think of falling off your bike many times or learning to do up your shoelaces. Yet suddenly as adults we expect to learn things on our first attempt. In a field that advocates so strongly the need for children to make mistakes and take risks in an appropriate environment, as adults we berate ourselves (and others) because we cannot do something the first time – or even after a few tries.

VAK learning

However you learn, the chances are that you will know how you learn best. Most of us at some point will have undertaken one of the many learning styles questionnaires to discover what type of learner we are. There are over 1.2 million websites devoted to 'learning style tests', so plenty to choose from if you have not had a go. Perhaps the most famous learning styles questionnaire was developed in 1986 by Honey and Mumford who discuss the following:

- pragmatist (plan)
- activist (do)
- reflector (review)
- theorist (conclude).

There are three main types of learning approaches – visual, auditory and kinaesthetic (tactile), normally known as VAK. It is useful to know how you learn – whether by using your own self-reflection about times when you were actively engaged in learning or by using one of the questionnaires.

- Are you a visual learner – do you like diagrams and remember what you see?
- Are you an auditory learner – do you remember what you heard and said?
- Are you a kinaesthetic learner – do you remember what you felt and touched; do you learn when you are doing something?
- Or, in fact, are you a combination of all three, depending on where you are and what you are engaged in?

The chances are that you will have one preferred learning approach and use the others as and when necessary. It is important to know how you learn as then you can also know when you do not learn or have difficulty learning and take steps to develop that area of your learning sphere. Reflecting on a recent training event attended – whether a formal training course, a short workshop, or a large conference – you may have seen the following behaviours exhibited:

- People who listened intently and wrote copious notes.
- People who played with their pen, necklace, etc.
- People who said nothing but later came up with suggestions.
- People who talked to their neighbour the whole way through.
- People who had something to say at every opportunity.
- People who appeared not to be interested, just noting the odd sentence.

The above are just some examples; you will be able to add others of your own. However, all of these people are exhibiting examples of their learning styles.

Visual learners tend to:

- Learn by writing everything down, which they may or may not need to read later.
- Learn by reading, watching video clips, watching others, etc.

Auditory learners tend to:

- Listen intently, then go away to think about what they have heard.
- Learn by verbalising, and so need to talk at regular intervals.

Kinaesthetic learners tend to:

- Learn better if they are physically moving, and if they cannot do so then will play with pens, etc.
- Write brief notes to look up later, so they are physically involved in their learning.

Thinking back to the training event/conference attended, was the trainer able to appeal to all these different people and their different styles of learning? On a training course where the trainer is acutely aware of individual learning styles, the course will be designed to appeal to a range of learners. There will be opportunities to read, video clips to watch, opportunities to listen and speak to the trainer and others in the group, and there will be role-play type activities or objects available that have a kinaesthetic or tactile quality. The course will vary in pace and speed, have a variety of activities to appeal to each VAK style and will have theoretical input as well as facilitator and group input.

How does this influence your role as a leader? If we know how others learn, then developing quality practitioners, and therefore quality practice, becomes an easier task. If, for example, you only ever give people written information and instructions, then how do the auditory and kinaesthetic learners 'hear' what you are saying? Taking team meetings as an example, the reflection point below gives you an opportunity to see how a team meeting can be facilitated.

Reflection: activity

Understanding learning styles – VAK

As a leader it is vital to understand how your team, and the individuals within your team, learn. You might want to ask the following in relation to team meetings:

- How do you organise them?

- How can you allow people to take risks, make and learn from mistakes?

- Do you think the VAK styles of learning involve everyone? How can you facilitate the meetings to incorporate VAK learning styles?

- Who can help ensure everyone is involved in these meetings?

- What else might you need to know or do?

To be open to learning we need to consider preferred learning styles, the emotional well-being of the learners, the physical environment in which the learning takes place and the need to provide opportunities to study our own learning/thinking.

More information can be found in Chapters 3 and 6. For more information on VAK learning you might want to try Gregorc (1985) or Dunn and Dunn (1998).

Learning is intrinsic in children: they are born 'programmed' to learn. As adults we can choose how we interact with our own learning. We can choose to be interested, involved and open to learning, or not. The opportunities to learn are everywhere, and do not have to be formal and in classrooms. Just watching an interesting television programme can constitute learning if we allow it to. The leader needs to ensure that learning is seen as a continuum, and should lead by example. How do your team see your interactions with learning? Do you embrace new ideas and opportunities, or are these seen as just one more thing that needs doing? As leaders we should be supporting teams to access a range of learning situations and opportunities, and also facilitate reflection following training. Moon (1999) talks of reflection taking place in a suitably conducive environment which contains, amongst other things:

> ... an emotionally supportive environment in which learners feel safe to take risks in their cognitive exploration.

> (Moon 1999, p. 161)

The Leader as a Learner values learning in its entirety. Throughout the setting learning is used positively to develop potential as well as to raise practice. Whether through reflection, feedback or more traditional methods, learning is embraced. In other words, leaders ensure that learning is seen as an integral part of quality improvement.

Chapter summary

This chapter looks at how leaders role model a positive approach to learning and help develop and facilitate a learning culture throughout the organisation. They do this by developing learning potential in themselves and in others. The giving and receiving of feedback is considered as a learning opportunity.

A successful leader provides an emotionally supportive environment in which teams and individuals feel safe to explore their thinking, ideas and practice. Reflection is embraced as a technique for learning in such a setting.

Finally, an awareness of individual learning styles can help support leadership. In effective organisations, learning experiences for both leaders and their teams are seen as valuable and are valued.

3 The Leader as an Enabler

If we all did the things we are capable of, we would astound ourselves.

(Thomas Edison)

The Leader as an Enabler

Effective leaders support their teams to deliver high-quality services by finding out what helps and what hinders practice. They support practitioners to understand their roles and responsibilities and empower them to self-regulate and to suggest and implement improvement.

This chapter covers the leader's attitude and approach to the role of leading others and facilitating positive outcomes. As a leader or manager you cannot be everywhere at once. Your team need to know what is expected of them by the organisation, by your stakeholders and by law. You need to be able to trust them to deliver a high-quality service at all times, reflect on their practice and identify areas of strength as well as areas to develop. The staff team need to feel trusted and be confident that they know what is expected of them. They must be able to ask for support in order to understand the roles and responsibilities necessary to deliver a high-quality service. They need to feel confident to be able to reflect on their practice, suggest improvements and try things out, even when not always successful. They need to hear when you think they are doing a good job and also need to be able to praise their peers when they observe good practice within the workplace. Having a team of people who are self-regulating, reflective and able to achieve Continuous Quality Improvement (CQI) indicates a leader who is to enabling the above.

Servant leadership

The idea of 'servant leadership' was coined by Robert K. Greenleaf in the 1970s. His philosophy of leadership is little known in the early years education and childcare and playwork sectors but is highly regarded in business. For example, servant leader Howard Behar (2007) has written a book about the leadership principles that he used to build the Starbucks coffee shops empire.

Given that the majority of the early years and playwork workforce is female and that devolved forms of leadership are much more in line with what are seen as the traditionally female traits of caring and nurturing, it is perhaps surprising that servant leadership is largely unknown in this field.

Greenleaf discussed the idea of the 'servant as leader' in an essay first published in 1970. In it he states:

> *The servant-leader is servant first.... It begins with the natural feeling that one wants to serve, to serve first ... The difference manifests itself in the care taken by the servant – first to make sure that other people's highest priority needs are being served. The best test, and difficult to administer, is: Do those served grow as persons? Do they, while being served, become healthier, wiser, freer, more autonomous, more likely themselves to become servants?*

(www.greenleaf.org)

The term 'servant leader' does not refer to an overworked skivvy who has to do everything. It should be viewed in a positive way. As leaders we have a purpose to serve not only our teams, but our parents and families too. It does not mean that leaders should be 'all things to all people'. In fact, it means the opposite: that leaders need to 'serve' others and, in doing so, empower these others to 'serve' themselves.

Parallels between the needs of adults and children

The idea of leaders meeting the needs and interests of their staff can be compared to child-led education. In early years settings, children experience much deeper levels of learning, higher levels of motivation and longer periods of perseverance and concentration when their own needs and interests are followed and they are engaged in episodes of sustained shared thinking. This does not mean that the adults are detached from the child's experience, far from it; they provide a rich and stimulating learning environment within a strong and supportive emotional environment in order to achieve the best outcomes for children. Within the balance of child-led: adult-led early years provision the adult has an important role to play in providing the support and challenge required to meet the individual needs of all children.

As an enabler, the leader acknowledges that practitioners have needs and interests too. A good leader knows his/her people: their strengths, their weaknesses, their interests. Enabling leadership does not mean that the needs and interests of the children or the organisation are subsumed by the needs and interests of the practitioners. It means that the needs and interests of the practitioners are recognised and taken into consideration. The balance of support and challenge and the importance of the physical as well as the emotional environment is key. The enabling or caring leader must be able to establish the needs of the practitioners and whether they have been met. Just like the children the practitioners are responsible for, some needs will be physical, some emotional, some related to development, some very individual and others generic.

Examples of physical needs include comfort, warmth, safety, a pleasant (perhaps aesthetically pleasing) work environment, proper breaks and being paid correctly and on time (to enable other physical comforts and responsibilities). These needs are fairly easy to manage and our effectiveness in carrying them out is a tangible demonstration of the care we provide for those we lead. Again, this can be linked to the needs of children, as outlined in the work of Ferre Laevers and others (2005). Laevers advocates the importance of well-being in children. In his work on SICS (a process-oriented Self-evaluation Instrument for Care Settings) he offers the following observations.

Well-being

- children with a high level of well-being *feel* great
- they *enjoy* life to the full

- they have *fun*, take joy in each other and in their surroundings
- they radiate *vitality* as well as relaxation and *inner peace*
- they adopt an *open* and *receptive* attitude towards their environment
- they are *spontaneous* and can fully be themselves
- well-being is linked to *self-confidence*, a good degree of *self-esteem* and *resilience*
- all this is based on *being in touch with themselves*, with their own feelings and experiences, fresh and pure.

(For more information, see Laever and others 2005, or the English pages on the Dutch website for childcare in Flanders – www.kindengezin.be)

This is what we should also want for staff. As an enabling or caring leader, we should be supporting the well-being of our staff (as well as our children), in other words, ensuring their emotional needs are being met in the workplace. These needs are best established during the recruitment process, through appraisal and through day-to-day communication and open-door practices. To ensure that these needs are being met you may have a range of checks, audits, observations, questionnaires, reviews, appraisals, etc.

Examples of emotional needs might include:

- being and feeling valued
- feeling able to try things out in an atmosphere of security
- feeling supported when things do not go as well as hoped
- feeling able to suggest ideas and opinions
- feeling involved and part of a team
- being recognised for work done well and feeling able to ask for help when needed.

Although not tangible, this list demonstrates in a much stronger way the care we provide for those we lead. It is about the culture that we as leaders create.

Additionally, you need to be aware of other needs that may be specific to individual practitioners, for example, training and development needs, managing disability, cultural or religious needs or family circumstances.

We have established that your staff team have needs and that as a leader you have some responsibility for caring for them and identifying and meeting those needs. However, it is possible that you could create a wonderful environment where everyone feels cared for but where they are so bored or so busy that they seem to get nothing done well or are unable to do so without instruction. You may have observed examples such as these with both adults and children in early years and playwork settings. With children we are looking to encourage participation, independence and choice in order to foster self-esteem and a good disposition and attitude to learning for life. This is not far removed from our aspirations for adults working in early years and playwork settings. We want adults who enjoy their work, who are able to plan, carry out and evaluate the effectiveness of their work, who are able to identify and implement improvements within the organisation and who continue to learn. Continuing the parallel of child-led education, the leader has an important role to play in providing the support and challenge required to meet the individual needs of all practitioners.

Motivation and the opposite of motivation

Praise should always be given in public; criticism should always be given in private.

(J. Paul Getty)

A phrase often repeated is that leaders need to 'motivate their workers' (also see Chapter 6). However this is done, it is equally important to reflect on what de-motivates your team and try your best to eliminate it. There are external factors that could influence motivation: threatened job cuts, funding and difficulty in recruiting, but we are focusing here on internal factors that leaders and managers can influence.

Reflection: activity

Personal motivation

Think about times that you have felt particularly motivated – this could be in your work or private life. Now consider times when you have felt particularly de-motivated. Repeat this exercise with your family, friends or work colleagues. Below are some questions that might help get you going:

- What was the situation?
- How did you feel at the beginning?
- Why were you motivated?
- What was the outcome?
- Was any reward involved?
- How did you feel afterwards?

De-motivation

As the opposite of motivation

It should be apparent that whilst we are motivated by different things and to different extents by similar things, there are some themes that emerge: for example, themes around encouragement and support, opportunity and challenge. The themes for de-motivation are often the opposite. Below are some examples, but you will probably have some of your own; motivation and de-motivation are often themed, but are personal and individual too.

How to de-motivate people:

- never saying thank you
- telling lies and never admitting to anything
- being pessimistic and negative
- being ambiguous in everything you say
- giving too many instructions and expecting things to be done immediately
- making too many rules
- naming and shaming whenever someone makes a mistake

- never tackling issues amongst staff
- never being available for your team
- never saying 'I do not know'
- never saying 'I was wrong'.

Think of the leaders and managers you have worked with previously who left you feeling frustrated; the chances are they would have displayed some of the traits cited in the list above and you could probably add a few more besides. Thinking about your own teams: Do you stray into the list occasionally, however unintentionally? Do your teams and the individuals in them get frustrated and, if so, how can you help? This is where the enabling leader can excel: combating frustration.

Combating frustration

Think of the things that frustrate you and how these lead to de-motivation. They are usually simple things that get in the way of doing your job effectively and efficiently, for example, an unreliable photocopier or the fact that there is never any paper in it when you want to use it. These things are not usually difficult to put right, they are just hassles.

The phrase 'hassle-free management' was first coined by the 1950s quality guru Philip Crosby (Crosby 1984). It is a simple idea: first find out what hassles your team have that prevent them from doing their job well, then work together to fix them. The result of this should be more than increased efficiency or effective working practices; it should translate to the workforce feeling more valued. Because they feel listened to they are more likely to report other hassles. Because they have been involved in finding a collective solution they are more likely to offer solutions as well as report problems in the future. If there is no immediate answer to the problem, at least it has been acknowledged as an issue, and although it may still be frustrating the damaging effects of de-motivation may be held at bay. This is a recipe for Continuous Quality Improvement (CQI) for the entire team.

Reflection: activity

Managing hassle through staff meetings

One of the best places to start managing hassle is with a team meeting, explaining the concept, setting the ground rules and inviting comment.

Hassles might be collected in writing or verbally, via a book or notice in the staff room, through smaller team meetings or in full staff meetings.

Ground rules should also include how hassles relating to individual people should be reported and dealt with. This process should make your team feel empowered, not threatened.

The case study below looks at an everyday situation in a busy childcare setting.

 ## Reflection: case study

Managing hassle

In a large nursery there are four people working in the Jelly Baby Room, a twelve-place room for children aged between eighteen and twenty-four months. Staff breaks are scheduled for fifteen minutes each between 10am and 11am. A practitioner reports that she is regularly missing out on her break. On investigation it turns out that there are several hassles.

- The first break does not often begin on time at 10am. There are a number of suggested reasons for this:

  o Nappy changing (conveyor belt style) starts at 9:30am and is not always finished in the half-hour, especially if it starts late.

  o Not noticing the time especially if working in the outdoor area.

  o Not wanting to have breaks too early especially if working a late shift.

- By the time a member of staff has taken the kettle to the kitchen, filled it with water and returned to the staff room and boiled it, at least five and often ten minutes will have elapsed.

  o Staff do not think this is fair to the person on break first and some count their fifteen minutes from when the kettle has boiled; others omit to refill the kettle ready for the next person.

    ○ Some subsequent members of staff take twenty and sometimes twenty-five minutes for their break.

    ○ This is not explained or apologised for at the time so some staff feel less valued than others but none of the staff feel able to challenge those taking longer breaks.

At 11am one qualified member of staff from this room is always expected to cover an early lunch break in the baby room.

Finding solutions

As we are distanced from the example, it is easy to spot some of the glaring causes and effects that have resulted in this particular hassle. The staff themselves have suggested some of the causes and thereby inferred some easy solutions to the problems. As a leader or manager it might be very tempting to tell the team how to tackle the situation, but that would probably not offer a lasting solution or foster the kind of behaviour you would want to encourage, namely reflective practice and problem solving.

There would be little point in this book giving a solution to the hassle described above, because every organisation is different and what works in one organisation (context) may not work in another. Leadership is a game of good judgement; knowing when to step in and when to hold back, whether to tackle the large or the small issues first and in what order. What the enabling leader does is support the workforce in understanding the situation, first by agreeing a description of the problem, perhaps by making notes on a flipchart, perhaps by organising further investigation, then helping the team analyse why it has occurred and the effect it has had. Finally, the enabling leader, in possession of the same knowledge as the workforce, supports them to find solutions, to prioritise actions and to monitor the implementation of them with a good dose of encouragement, support and challenge. The enabling leader does not do the job for the workforce but removes hassles and models good practice so that the workforce can manage problems and identify improvements independently.

de Bono's Six Thinking Hats

Another way of managing differences of opinions and hassles and encouraging creative thinking within a team is by using Edward de Bono's 'Six Thinking Hats' (1985) method. The official de Bono website describes the approach:

> The principle behind the 'Six Thinking Hats' is parallel thinking which ensures that all the people in a meeting are focused on and thinking about the same subject at the same time.

The idea behind de Bono's approach is that all team members concentrate on one colour of hat at the same time.

The Six Hats

The White Hat *calls for information known or needed: 'The facts, just the facts'*

The Yellow Hat *symbolises brightness and optimism, allowing you to explore the positives and probe for value and benefit*

The Black Hat *signifies caution and critical thinking, why something may not work – do not overuse*

The Red Hat *signifies feelings, hunches and intuition – the place where emotions are placed without explanation*

The Green Hat *focuses on creativity, possibilities, alternatives and new ideas; it offers the opportunity to express new concepts and new perceptions – lateral thinking could be used here*

The Blue Hat *is used to manage the thinking process and ensures that the 'Six Thinking Hats' guidelines are observed*

(www.edwdebono.com)

You could introduce de Bono's hats in much the same way as described in the reflection point on managing hassles through team meetings. The principles are the same. Introduce the different colours of hats, with explanations for each one, and then invite comments, concentrating on one colour at a time. Encourage each member of the team to say at least one thing for each colour of hat.

A cautionary note

Inviting your workforce to let you know the problems within your organisation means that you have to be prepared to do something about it. Picture the practitioner who knows there is a problem, has some good (or poor) ideas about what could be done to improve the situation and a manager who cannot or will not discuss or implement the ideas. That will lead to a frustrated (and ultimately de-motivated) practitioner.

Hassle-free management is about the hassles as perceived by your staff team. These hassles may not be your top priorities but they matter to your team and helping to find solutions will improve their work experience, increase their motivation and, ultimately, may even make your improvement priorities easier to introduce. The 'hassle' slot on the staff meeting agenda should not just be a list of your gripes. It is primarily for the staff to air their issues. Be prepared to admit your mistakes or take responsibility for the effect that things you have done or not done may have had on the organisation and be prepared to make changes (see also Chapter 2, particularly the sections on Reflection and the Johari Window).

John Adair (1998, p. 103) offers a following short course for leadership, which would be useful to bear in mind when considering de-motivation and frustration within your team:

The 6 most important words ... 'I admit I made a mistake.'

The 5 most important words ... 'I am proud of you.'

The 4 most important words ... 'What is your opinion?'

The 3 most important words ... 'If you please.'

The 2 most important words ... 'Thank you.'

The 1 most important word ...   'We.'

The least important word ...   'I.'

If this seems a little 'touchy–feely', think about the leaders and managers you admire, as well as the ones you do not. Which ones use words from the above list?

Ability and capacity

Ability refers to a person's skills or qualities. Capacity refers to the amount, level or potential of work/learning a person is able to do. There are of course other factors that influence ability and capacity, such as the environment, resources and personal issues. This is another important concept for the enabling leader and is linked to hassle-free management. When addressing poor quality in a practitioner's work, the leader needs to ask two questions:

1. Has this person the *ability* to do this element of their role well? (Have they the skills/knowledge/understanding to undertake the task?)

2. Has this person the *capacity* to do this element of their role well? (Have they the amount of time needed, the resources necessary or the potential to learn, in order to undertake the task?)

If the answer to the first question is no, then the leader needs to consider whether the situation can be improved, for example, by using methods such as training, coaching or mentoring.

If the answer to the first question is yes, but the second one is no, the leader needs to explore the causes of this.

In other words, people may be able to do a given task, but are you enabling them to undertake the task? When individuals are unable to undertake their job roles, despite support and training, there may be issues of capability: this is explored further in Chapter 7.

Lack of time is something that is often cited as affecting a person's capacity to do a job well. A practitioner may be very able in terms of planning next steps for a child – however, if only given half an hour's non-contact time per week (and that only when no-one is sick, away training or on holiday) in which to catch up on records as well as plan, it is highly likely that the planning will be a long way from perfect. As a leader and as an organisation you will need to decide how near to perfect is necessary and acceptable for each type of task and when only perfect will do. You will also need to look carefully at ways to increase or maximise people's capacity to perform their job roles to the best of their ability, and that may mean managing the additional jobs you give some people, perhaps by taking away other responsibilities or by monitoring and ensuring that non-contact time is given when promised.

Resources are another frequent source of discontent with regard to a person's capacity to do a job. Difficulty in accessing a computer is one example, lack of appropriate equipment another and, perhaps more frequently, poorly organised or poorly stored equipment. Practitioners often complain that when they want to use a piece of equipment it either cannot be found, a piece is missing or that someone else is using it.

Addressing capacity issues caused by hassles can increase an individual's job satisfaction. By acknowledging and discussing ability and capacity issues the enabling leader can support the practitioner to reflect on the quality of practice, identify the things that are preventing or impeding good practice and thereby make changes to improve the efficiency and or effectiveness of the service being delivered.

Empowering the team, safeguarding the organisation

Enabling leaders recognise that although they may be an integral part of the organisation, perhaps the public face of the organisation or the owner/founder of the business, they are not 'the organisation'. The organisation is an entity in its own right. For a variety of reasons, key personnel within an organisation may sometimes leave. Sometimes this can be planned for, but sometimes the reasons are dramatic or tragic and there is little or no warning. In the absence of the leader, the organisation should still be able to continue and flourish. To do this successfully requires a strong capable team who are sure of their roles and responsibilities and good succession management, ensuring that all key management responsibilities can be carried out by more than one person. Enabling leaders do not see themselves as omnipotent powers but seek a devolved power. They share the trials and the triumphs of the organisation with the team and, most importantly, share information and involve the team in decision making.

The enabling leader makes it their business to get the best out of everyone by nurturing, encouraging, coaching and mentoring. Like giving a ten-month-old a spoon to have a go themselves or giving a two-year-old a dustpan and brush to clear up the sand, you know that the result might not be perfect and that your help will probably be required, but you also know that valuable learning is taking place and you see the satisfaction when a new skill is achieved. Enabling leaders support and challenge their staff teams to achieve new skills, often knowing that they could have done it twice as well in half the time. It takes a far stronger individual to do this than to hold on to all knowledge and, ultimately, power.

Chapter summary

This chapter looks at how the leader functions as an enabler within an organisation. This is done by creating a culture of shared responsibility within the organisation, where teams are self-regulating, reflective and feel able to suggest and try out new ways of working, even when they are not always successful.

Such a leader is mindful of the individual's well-being and takes care to meet the needs and interests of the staff team in order to empower them to deliver quality services.

The chapter goes on to deal with some of the causes of motivation and de-motivation in the workplace, the latter often leading to frustration. The concept of 'hassle-free management' is then introduced as a way of trying to combat the resultant frustration.

Enabling leaders support and challenge their teams to manage problems and identify improvements independently. Additionally, they look for ways to improve an individual's ability and capacity to carry out their roles.

Successful leaders devolve power and develop leadership and management throughout the team to ensure the long term survival of the organisation.

4 The Leader as a Mentor

A mentor is someone who allows you to
see the hope inside yourself.

(Oprah Winfrey)

The Leader as a Mentor

Effective leaders use techniques and approaches traditionally associated with
mentoring (and the associated disciplines), such as developing autonomy, supporting
reflection and offering challenge.

In the previous chapter we looked at how the enabling leader
supports the staff team to develop skills and find their own solutions
to problems. One way of facilitating this is to employ a mentoring
approach. This chapter will begin to explore how the skills,
knowledge and experiences that are traditionally associated with
mentoring can support the people who work with and around us.

There are several definitions and a range of understandings of
mentoring, including a wealth of documentation, research and
practice that describes and uses this type of approach. There is also
a range of terminology used for the associated disciplines, for
example, buddying, coaching, counselling and peer-support. They
each use some or all of the traits that will be explored within this
chapter. For the purpose of this book the terms used will be
'mentor' for the person offering the support, 'mentoring' for the
nature of that support and 'mentee' for the individual, group or
setting to whom the support is offered. This chapter looks at the
skills associated with mentoring and how these may help in the
leadership role.

Many people assume that 'mentoring' is a new concept, probably
American, and a product of the go-getting, stronger, faster

initiatives of the late-twentieth century. The word 'mentor', however, has its origins in Greek mythology. Odysseus had appointed his young son Telemachus to oversee his kingdom whilst he was away fighting in the Trojan War. Before leaving for war, Odysseus approached his good friend Mentor to advise Telemachus and support him until such time as he returned. The idea, then, of a person acting as 'wise counsel' is actually much older than was initially thought.

Definitions of mentoring and associated disciplines

There is much debate about the difference between coaching, buddying, mentoring and counselling, and much variance in terms of a true definition. For the purpose of this book, the following assumptions have been made:

- Counselling tends to concentrate on personal development where there is a specific problem to be solved.
- Buddying tends to be peer support with someone who works in a similar situation and can also be referred to as peer-mentoring or peer-coaching.
- Coaching tends to be about skills, and supporting a person to get to where they want to be (think of sports coaches).
- Mentoring tends to be about supporting a person to find their own answers in a safe, supportive but appropriately challenging environment (that is, developing autonomy).

Coaching, mentoring and buddying tend to concentrate on work, education and professional development. That is not to say that, for example, counselling never strays into professional areas for development or indeed that mentoring never considers personal concerns: a true definition is elusive.

The Coaching and Mentoring Network, a web-based news, information and resource centre for anyone involved in mentoring and coaching, offers the following definition:

Coaching and mentoring:

- *actively untaps potential*

- *fine tunes and develops skills*

- *utilises development activities designed to suit the client's personal needs and learning styles*

- *eliminates specific performance problems*

- *can focus on interpersonal skills, which cannot be readily or effectively transferred in a traditional training environment*

- *provides the client with contacts and networks to assist with furthering their career or life aspirations*

- *is performed in the 'live' environment*

- *is highly effective when used as a means of supporting training initiatives to ensure that key skills are transferred to the 'live' environment*

- *advocates coaches and mentors transferring the skills to the client rather than doing the job for them.*

(www.coachingnetwork.org.uk)

It should be apparent from this definition that 'coaching' and 'mentoring' are often used interchangeably.

This chapter looks at how these skills can support leadership. In reality the lines are blurred and it probably does not matter which definition you use, as long as you know which role you are in and why. Many of the skills associated with traditional mentoring can equally be applied to the role of leader, and can actively support leaders to have confidence in their ability to carry out their role.

Mentoring in practice

Mentoring can be many things; it can be informal (for example, where you speak to a colleague or a friend about an issue or concern), or formal (where you are assigned a mentor as part of work or training, for example). It can be self-chosen, mutually agreed upon or imposed. It may be that you choose your own mentor, someone whose opinions and thoughts you respect and value, or it may be that someone offers to be your mentor.

If you are in a position of being able to choose a mentor, you should look for someone who will challenge your thinking appropriately, ask relevant and useful questions and listen to you. Therefore, it might not be appropriate to choose a person who you know will instantly agree with everything you say and tell you that everything you do is wonderful! It may be that you and a colleague decide to mentor each other whilst experiencing similar situations, such as developing a new project or managing and leading a team through change (this is often referred to as peer-mentoring or buddying).

Mentoring can sometimes feel imposed, such as being given a mentor as part of an induction or a training programme, regardless of whether you feel you need one or not. In this situation it is worth remembering that mentoring is intended to be a positive experience, to help you organise your thoughts, and that many people (even those who are originally sceptical) find mentor sessions worthwhile and extremely valuable.

The mentoring relationship could be one where power is balanced (i.e., between two colleagues) or where there is an imbalance of power (i.e., between a leader and member of staff). Just as the definitions above show the confusion in finding a true and agreed distinction between mentoring/coaching, etc., similarly, there is uncertainty in the power balance of a mentor–mentee relationship. In some circles mentors are seen as the experts or 'wise counsels'. Elsewhere, the relationship is regarded as equal, with the mentee having a vision for their own goals and desires and possibly needing help in clarifying thoughts and next steps. This also applies to coaching, which can be seen as an expert–novice relationship or an equal partnership.

Whatever wording you use or definition you adopt, adapt or develop, and whether or not the relationship is equal, is almost irrelevant. It is the quality of the dialogue that is most important. In other words, what is crucial is what takes place when you discuss issues, goals, desires, situations or concerns.

Mentoring or leadership?

Consider how the skills, knowledge, understanding, experiences and qualities required in formal and informal mentoring can be transferred to leadership roles. Think about the following quotes about mentoring. Could they apply to leadership? If you replace the word 'mentor' with the word 'leader' do they still make sense?

> *Mentors who seek consultation from trusted colleagues are consistently more likely to make better decisions than those who do not.*
>
> (Johnson and Ridley 2004, p. 87)

Shea, in his book *Mentoring: A Guide to the Basics* (1992), discusses seven types of mentor assistance:

1. Helping a person to shift his/her mental context

2. Listening when the mentoree has a problem

3. Identifying mentoree feelings and verifying them (feedback)

4. Effectively confronting negative intentions or behaviour

5. Providing appropriate information when needed

6. Delegating authority or giving permission

7. Encouraging the exploration of options

(Shea 1992, p. 43)

If we use the theory about mentoring and apply it to the leadership role, then the leader as a mentor:

- asks questions
- listens
- develops autonomy
- supports others to make decisions
- supports others to lead
- delegates
- gives permission
- offers praise and encouragement
- allows for mistakes (from which to learn)

- seeks advice from colleagues
- offers challenges
- supports reflection.

Mentoring is not the only way to lead a team, in the same way that none of the other chapters/leadership skills in this book are standalone. The key message here is that the skills associated with mentoring are easily transferable to parts of your leadership role.

Reflection: case study

The following case study assesses how mentoring, coaching, buddying or leadership skills can help a member of staff.

Mentor support

Anju has recently been appointed deputy manager of a new setting. As part of the new role, Anju is expected to undertake a relevant degree qualification. Anju is beginning to feel the pressure as she tries to find her feet in the new role. This is partly due to the time constraints of managing the setting and the staff she is responsible for, as well as completing the necessary work.

Anju has several avenues of help available to her. She could:

- talk to her line manager

- talk to a peer in a similar role

- talk to her friend who has been a deputy for many years

- request a mentor from the organisation

- talk to her best friend who manages a retail team in a department store.

Each option will have a range of benefits, but could also have a range of disadvantages. What Anju needs is someone with the appropriate skills to help channel her thoughts, decide on what options/actions to take and move forward. Given the mentoring skills highlighted previously, all of these are key in a mentor relationship, but apply equally to the role of leader.

However, could they also be applied to peer support, or perhaps the support offered by a friend? There is no right or wrong answer to this – what is needed is the appropriate skill set. Consider each source of support available to Anju and the skills the person might have to be able to support her. Now consider the disadvantages. Below are a few examples:

Role	Benefits	Disadvantages
Line manager	May be able to support Anju to take risks/make mistakes	
Peer	May understand the support needed as they have been through similar situation	
Friend in a deputy role at a different setting		May not be able to ask questions that are helpful and relevant
Friend in retail management		May not have knowledge of the context
Mentor	Can challenge appropriately	

Developing mentor skills for the leadership role

Many of the skills required to mentor effectively, such as listening, challenging appropriately, permitting risk taking, allowing for mistakes and using questioning are equally valid in the leadership role. This next section looks at some of those key skills in more detail.

Communication skills

Good communication skills are vital in a mentoring relationship. As well as speaking and listening, asking questions, and body language, other things that can influence our ability to communicate include, for example, the venue. Holding a mentor session in a busy office or café may affect the outcome for the mentee. Mentoring meetings can take place in a range of settings – in the workplace of either person, on mutually agreed ground or on neutral ground. A general agreement is that mentoring is best suited to neutral ground, which helps reduce any power imbalance and minimises the risk of constant interruptions. In the workplace, you need to ensure as leader that conversations happen at appropriate times and places and that your team has somewhere to talk to each other, as well as to you.

Feelings and emotions can also influence how we communicate. Although mentoring is not strictly about feelings and emotions, there will be times when we need help to organise our feelings and emotions about professional situations. Likewise, there may be times when feelings and emotions obstruct our thought process (see also Chapter 2, on reflection). At times like these it can be useful to have someone independent to talk to, someone who listens and hears, and someone who can help clarify your thoughts. This is when a mentor session can be invaluable. As a leader you need to consider who your team can turn to in order to think things through.

Listening/hearing

Listening is the most important skill in terms of mentoring and communication. While mentoring, the mentor should spend much of the time listening whilst the mentee does most of the talking. Sometimes someone will say they are listening but continue with other activities. Listening is about actively engaging with what you have heard and paying due attention to what is being said, for example:

- Questioning (how did that make you feel?).
- Checking back (what I am hearing is …).
- Clarifying (it sounds to me like you …).

Think about a discussion you have had recently where you were looking for help.

- Who did most of the talking?
- Did you feel helped?
- Did you feel you had things left to say?

And perhaps most importantly

- Did you feel listened to?

Quite often when we ask for help, we are given a range of solutions, options and advice as to what the other person would do had they been in our shoes. This is sometimes useful (if you are looking for ideas you had not thought of), but it does not help you to explore possibilities yourself.

Using questioning

In terms of mentoring, questioning is often quoted as being one of the key skills. In reality, we do not always know what questions to ask or where to begin. A good starting point is to think of the old adage 'Do as you would be done by'. It is important not to fire questions rapidly at people, as that could make even the most confident person uncomfortable. Allowing the other person time to consider their answers, being prepared to clarify and, if you do not understand, then saying so, are some other useful ways in which to conduct a successful mentoring session. As for where to start, it is useful to have a bank of generic questions in your head. Most questions begin with one of the same six words:

- who
- what
- where
- when
- why
- how.

Reflection: activity

Questioning

Try practising this in a safe environment, for instance, with your children when they get in from school or with a friend who has just returned from holiday. There are 'standard questions' that open up dialogue and conversation and it is useful to have a few of these up your sleeve. For example:

- Tell me more about …

- What ideas have you got on this?

- How do you see this working out?

- Why do you want to be involved?

- Who could help you?

- I'm listening, but am not sure I understand, so tell me what you need …

Any of these questions should offer a chance to open up dialogue. They can also help if there is conflict, or you are not sure what to do in order to help, and you need a bit of breathing space to gather your thoughts. It is useful when you first start using this technique to have a few written down that you can quickly read through before you go into a meeting; later you will find that the who, what, where, when, why, how and tell me … become almost mantra-like in your head.

Some of these prefixes will give you one-word answers, so you need to phrase your questions appropriately in order to encourage dialogue. There are other ways of enquiring: 'Can you tell me about …', 'Explain to me about …' being good examples but, whichever form you use, you need to be comfortable with asking the question.

The GROW model of solving problems and realising goals

The GROW model is another form of using questioning to focus ideas, problem solve and move towards goals. The model has been developed by a host of people including Sir John Whitmore (2002). It is widely used in coaching situations and therefore an exact source is difficult to define. The information discussed here has been adapted from the work of Bob Griffiths, and can be found in his book *GROW Your Own Carrot* (2004) and on his website (www.bobgriffiths.com).

The idea behind the GROW model is a stepped approach in tackling issues, solving problems, identifying and realising goals and being able to identify and track progress. The initials stand for the stages of GROW, which are:

Goal,
Reality,
Obstacles/Options, and
Way Forward.

The GROW model is a simple, straightforward way of thinking about each step along the way in thoughtful detail. Questions are used as a way of developing specific phrases that help to assist you in moving forwards. Below are some of the questions available in the GROW model used by Bob Griffiths, but many more are available. These questions illustrate how the GROW model could be used in either a leadership or mentoring capacity:

Goal
The Goal stage is about where you want to be, or what you want to do. They help to give your thoughts focus and give you something to aim for. Questions at this stage could include:

- Is my Goal of a manageable size and not too big?
- Is my Goal largely within my competence and control?
- Is my Goal measurable?

Reality

The Reality stage looks at where you are now, how you feel about your current situation and what you might need to help you achieve your goal. Questions here could include:

- What steps do I need to complete to achieve my Goal?
- Have I included the relevant facts and figures?
- Have I included my feelings about my current situation?

Obstacles and Options

The Obstacles stage looks at what is stopping you from reaching your Goal. Options should help you to remove or negotiate the Obstacles. Questions at this stage could include:

- What is blocking the achievement of the Goal? What evidence is there for this?
- What is the simplest way around the Obstacles?
- Are there past experiences that can help with this situation?
- Are there enough Options to move forward?

Way Forward

The Way Forward stage looks at what you need to do next, using the SMART (Specific, Measurable, Achievable, Relevant, Timed) format as a way of measuring and monitoring progress.

- What is the first step and what is the last?
- Who might be able to help?
- Are the actions needed SMART?

Reflection: activity

Using the questions above (plus any additional ones you create yourself), how would you use the GROW model to help Matt deal with the following situation? Using the following grid, note down any questions you could ask Matt. Use the final column for any thoughts you have.

A staff meeting is due to start in five minutes. Sarah, the manager, is on the phone ordering some new equipment. Of the six other staff in the setting, two are in the staff room having a coffee, three are tidying the rooms and one is putting up a display. Matt comments that team meetings are not a priority and that no-one ever turns up on time. Matt sighs and says he wishes he could take over running the team meetings and then people might see how important and useful they could be.

What is the GOAL ...?

Stage	Question	Thoughts
Goal		
Reality		
Obstacles		
Options		
Way Forward		

By using the GROW model we can see that:

Matt's Goal is for people to see the benefit of team meetings.

The Reality is that Matt is motivated to organise the meetings and can see their benefit, but may need support from his colleagues.

The Obstacle could be Sarah: how does the manager feel about someone else leading the team meetings and how does Matt motivate the other staff?

The Options could be either to trial Matt leading the team meetings or move the day/time when the meetings are scheduled.

The Way Forward could be to begin by discussing with each team member what they would like to see happen at team meetings.

This is a fairly simple example, and you may well have come up with different thoughts and questions to the ones used here. The GROW model can assist you to use traditional mentoring questioning skills in a leadership situation. In a mentor relationship, the GROW model could be used to support Matt to approach his manager with suggestions for a way forward. In a leadership situation, the GROW model could be used by Matt and Sarah to develop and focus team meetings. In this situation, though Matt is not the manager he is showing the desire and enthusiasm to develop leadership skills – a good leader would support this. In many teams, meetings are chaired or facilitated by different members of staff on a rolling programme. This allows people to develop chairperson and facilitation skills in a safe environment. The manager is still present and can ultimately make any necessary decisions, but leadership skills are shared and developed throughout the team.

Risks and mistakes

Leaders need to support their team to take risks and make mistakes in a safe environment. It is a way of developing learning. Think about being worried about approaching a member of staff with an issue you have to discuss with them. In a mentor relationship, you would be able to safely try out different angles of approach, practise saying the difficult things in a range of ways and explore other options. In other words, you could make mistakes and take risks. As a leader, this is also what you want staff to be able to do. Think of supporting the member of staff who wants to try a heuristic play session with babies, or someone who would like to introduce role play to the outdoor area, or the person who is frightened of speaking to visitors: how can you as a leader support these people to try out ideas, take risks and make mistakes? The key point here is about the culture you create as a leader. Do you have no-blame culture, do your staff feel able to approach you with new ideas and suggestions (that is, take risks) and do you as a team learn from mistakes? (See also Chapter 2.)

Offering appropriate support and challenge

The word challenge often conjures up thoughts of difficulty, confrontation, test or fight. In the world of sport the word 'challenge' is used to refer to something not easy to complete: such as Rugby League's 'Challenge Cup', Motor Racing's 'World Rally Challenge' or Mountaineering's 'Three Peaks Challenge'. The implication of this everyday use of the word is that 'challenge' is difficulty and there needs to be a winner. In mentoring or leadership terms, 'challenge' needs to be seen differently. In this context, 'challenge' means to question or confront; as in an idea, issue or problem. The word 'confront' implies conflict, but confrontation in this case moderated by, as the title to this section states, the word 'appropriate'.

A good mentor, and indeed a good leader, has the skill to offer support and challenge in an appropriate way. Think of the different people you deal with every day, and how you support and challenge them in different ways; think about how you challenge the following situations and the skills you use to do this supportively:

- challenging an unfair decision by a senior manager
- challenging a racist remark made by a friend
- challenging a less experienced member of staff to create a display
- challenging a peer with developing a new project
- challenging a member of staff with persistent lateness.

With children, the Early Years Foundation Stage (EYFS) asks us to think about how we provide 'equipment and materials to maintain interest and provide challenge' (DfES 2007). Challenge here, is seen as being beneficial to the child, adding interest, and enhancing curiosity and learning. This is how leaders need to view the word 'challenge' and encourage staff to do so as well. As mentors and leaders we can then challenge appropriately in a range of situations.

Seeking support

Mindful mentors understand they have imperfections, limitations and weaknesses … they are honest about who they are as individuals … they are accustomed to thinking about their areas of vulnerability.

(Johnson and Ridley 2004, p. 87)

It may appear odd to have a quote about 'imperfections, limitations and weaknesses' and 'vulnerability' in a chapter that aims to help you become a more confident and effective leader. However, Johnson and Ridley also talk of the need to be 'mindful' and 'honest'. Though the above is a quote about mentoring, it can easily be applied to leadership. If we start with the premise that we hope to be 'mindful and honest', and that we cannot possibly know all things all of the time, then we must also accept that we have 'imperfections, limitations and weaknesses' and 'vulnerability'. Therefore, if this is the case, then mentoring skills can easily become an aspect of our leadership.

Good mentors and leaders recognise that we all need support occasionally. How do you ensure your staff have networks of support? Hopefully, staff will speak to you about most things, but there are also likely to be times when they would rather speak to someone else, for example, if they need support when applying for a promotion or other jobs. As a leader this is something you need to accept and encourage. If everyone wanted to speak directly and privately to you about every single idea, issue or concern they had, you would not have much time to do anything else.

It may be that you set up a mentor scheme within your setting, or that you access a scheme set up locally, or that you encourage and support the idea of staff finding their own sources of support outside of the workplace. Whichever way you decide to encourage your team to seek support, it is vital that everyone understands this is a professional relationship, for professional dialogue, as a means to channel thoughts to, for example, develop practice, move forward or raise confidence. One of the benefits often cited by leaders who have a professional mentor relationship is the luxury of having someone who is there 'just for you'.

Similarly, if you are to develop mentor skills in your leadership, you need to show staff that you believe in and advocate the use of mentoring in your workplace. Staff need to see that you too need support at times. Returning to the Johnson and Ridley quote, leaders need to recognise their 'limitations, imperfections and weaknesses' and become accustomed to thinking about 'areas of vulnerability'.

Johnson and Ridley also advocate that 'seeking consultation from trusted colleagues' assists with decision making. In other words we should all have our own support mechanisms. Think about your support networks, and who you turn to for peer support, who offers you support on leadership topics, where you go to for future career support and who listens to your hopes and dreams, worries and fears. Being a mentor and a leader can be both difficult and complex at times, and you need to ensure that you have a range of people you can turn to who will listen, question, allow you to take risks and make mistakes, and offer appropriate challenges. In other words you need to know who mentors you.

Chapter summary

This chapter sets out by seeking to understand the terminology used to describe mentoring and associated disciplines, such as counselling, coaching and buddying.

Mentoring relationships can be formal or informal. They can be between equals, for example between peers, or with people of greater experience.

The mentoring skill set, including active listening and questioning, can be used within the leadership role but is not the only way to lead.

Leaders need to develop a supportive environment and culture that enables appropriate risk taking and challenge.

They need to acknowledge their support and development needs, and should encourage and role model the use of supportive (mentoring) relationships.

5 The Leader as a Champion

If people were aware of what is at stake during the first few years of life, small children would be society's treasures …

(Rosa Maria Torres)

The Leader as a Champion

Effective leaders are ambassadors for their organisations. They have a vision that they develop and share with others. They act with integrity and lead by example, standing up for what they believe is right.

The previous chapters looked at how leaders, who are human, fallible and constantly learning in their profession, can serve and support their teams to reach their individual and organisational potential. This chapter will look at the Leader as a Champion. It does not abandon the idea of the 'human' but explores how leaders act as champions for children, their colleagues and the early years and playwork sectors. This chapter includes how leaders show support and champion through:

- the visions and values they hold and share
- their commitment to inclusion
- their involvement of others
- their commitment to quality.

The majority of people who work in early years and playwork do so because they passionately believe in helping to improve outcomes for children and families. For many, the roles long held include being an advocate for children, families and practitioners. This can start with small steps, such as allowing children to make choices during snack time, developing groups for parents to meet, and sharing ideas from training to support colleagues.

The word *'champion'* can either mean to be the best, to win and beat all rivals, or it can mean to fight on someone else's behalf. The Leader as a Champion is about the latter, about standing up for what is right in supporting others, whether children, families or colleagues in the sector. Part of the role of the Leader as a Champion is to ensure that everyone, including very young children, has a voice. Being a champion means ensuring that the organisation operates according to visions and values. It could mean supporting and implementing simple things such as continuous provision and access to outdoor areas for all children through to advocating rights in the workplace, such as the Working Time Directive.

Traits of the leader as a champion

The idea of 'champion' brings up thoughts of words such as:

- advocate
- rights
- ambassador
- spokesperson
- visionary.

The Leader as a Champion is someone who sets the tone for the organisation and who leads by example, being a role model in all aspects of their work. This is someone who can challenge, who is persistent, honest, open to ideas, and strong enough to stand up for what is right. These qualities apply both when operating within the organisation and also when working with the wider community.

A leader has the ability to stand up for a cause, for what is right, and to be principled. If you look back at Chapter 1, you will see that leaders do not have to be heroic or charismatic, with larger than life personalities. In fact, Mintzberg (1999) discusses the effectiveness of leaders who 'manage quietly'.

Think of the practitioner who attends a training course on heuristic play, returns to the team enthusiastic, asks to share the ideas at a team meeting, answers the questions, reassures those with doubts about health and safety, challenges the objections about risk and uses the EYFS to support the argument, researches and collates the resources, and then models a heuristic play session with a group of babies. That practitioner is leading, in a subtle and quiet way. Likewise, the practitioner is championing children's rights, quality practice and current thinking about how children learn and develop, again in a subtle and quiet way. Examples such as this occur daily in our working lives but are often not recognised and valued. Those of us in leadership roles should actively support and encourage such activity in order to help develop the leaders and champions of the future.

The qualities described above, such as being principled and being able to challenge, is not an exhaustive list. There will be things you want to add, alter and amend and there will be some aspects of your leadership you believe are more important than others. This might depend on the context within which you work or perhaps where you are on your leadership journey. Nevertheless, as in many aspects of life, balance is important and therefore it is also vital that you do not become too reliant on one aspect of leadership to the detriment of others.

Reflection: activity

Leaders you admire

There are many excellent leaders in the early years and playwork field. Think of the people you admire within this sector and beyond, those who lead with integrity and honesty, with passion and persistence. Think of leaders who stand up for what they believe in, challenge appropriately and thereby instigate change.

- Are they at the top of their professional ladder?

- Are they the most highly qualified?

- Are they passionate about their 'cause' or 'belief'?

- Do they influence development and change for the better?

In all probability, the answer to the first two questions will be 'no', but the answer to the last two questions will be 'yes'.

This also works with historical figures – think of the movements to abolish child labour and gain votes for women.

To understand the Leader as Champion it may be useful to look at who, what and why we are championing. The key stakeholders are:

- children
- families
- practitioners
- the setting (the organisation)
- other stakeholders – multi-disciplinary teams and so on
- early years and playwork field/profession.

It may well be that leaders in this field act as champions for some or all of the above, depending on job roles, experience and individual passions and causes. But what does the Leader as a Champion do? How do you act as a champion for the people you work with, for and alongside?

Within the organisation and sector, there are a range of documents, publications, policies and frameworks that support, provide reasoning and underpinning knowledge, and assist leaders to champion together with, or on behalf of, the key stakeholder groups above. Described below are four key areas of activity for the Leader as a Champion:

- values and vision
- inclusion
- involving others
- quality.

Championing values and vision

Values are not just words, values are what we live by. They're about the causes that we champion and the people we fight for.

(Senator John Kerry)

In the ELEYS study (2007, p. 21) Siraj-Blatchford and Manni say, 'The success of a setting is largely dependent upon the dedication, commitment and effort of the people within it.' The development and articulation of a shared vision and values is one way that leaders encourage this dedication, commitment and effort. Effective leaders support the development of a shared vision, encourage commitment to it and ensure all key stakeholders have ownership, understanding and awareness of their part in striving for and achieving the vision.

It may well be that the overarching vision is created elsewhere, by a corporate body, for example, but the skilful Leader as a Champion will support stakeholders to see how the vision can be interpreted at a local level and how it relates to their personal values, their individual roles and their setting. In creating the shared vision, leaders need to tune in to the personal values and vision of others and simultaneously support them to develop and clarify these whilst pulling together the threads to create a cohesive whole. Senge and others (2005, p. 133) call this drawing together process 'crystallizing intent'.

> *Crystallizing intent requires being open to the larger intention and imaginatively translating the intuitions that arise into concrete images and visions that guide action.*

Senge (2006, p. 203) talks about leaders enrolling others to the cause rather than trying to sell the idea. This implies an element of free will and choice that in turn leads to commitment rather than compliance and, therefore, a greater effort and willingness to achieve the vision by innovative means. Effective leaders do this by:

- facilitating the creation of a shared vision
- developing a vision that is appropriate, in line with personal and organisational values
- sharing and creating understanding
- enrolling others to the cause and gaining support to achieve the vision
- supporting others to understand where they are in relation to the desired vision; the current reality
- celebrating achievements in pursuit of the vision.

Leaders as story tellers

In order to make sustained and incremental improvements towards a desired vision of the future, leaders need to be able to support others to understand the current reality, what the new reality will be and how, collectively, they might get there. The ability of the leader to express this in words and pictures is important. Friedman (2005, p. 41) suggests story telling as a way for stakeholders to offer their different perspectives on the current reality and how it came to be. He says:

> Telling stories is the oldest form of communication, the oldest form of retained knowledge, and the oldest way in which we transform life experiences into useful lessons. The idea of telling stories allows each partner to explain her or his perspective on how we got where we are today.

As organisations move away from the old reality towards the new, leaders tell and re-tell the story. Cuno (2005, p. 205) quotes Howard Gardner who 'calls these stories "stories of identity", narratives "that help individuals think about and feel who they are, where they come from, and where they are headed" and that such stories "constitute the single most powerful weapon in the leader's literary arsenal"'.

In order to reach the new reality, the 'concrete images and vision' referred to above are more likely to be achieved if they can be described with clarity and unity by the leader and others. Effective leaders are able to paint a vivid picture of that new reality in terms of how things will look, how people will feel, what they will be doing, and so on. Effective communication skills therefore have a direct bearing on the ability to influence vision and values and, therefore, the commitment, rather than just the compliance of the team.

Championing inclusion

Leaders should ensure that all key stakeholders, including children, other service users and practitioners, feel included, valued and are consulted. For the Leader as a Champion this is about true inclusion and not just about paying lip service to a few 'target' groups. Such a leader ensures that all parts of the local and professional community are involved in the development of the setting. The Leader as a Champion at all times considers:

- equality of opportunity
- anti-discriminatory practice
- valuing diversity
- disability or special educational needs
- barriers to inclusion.

There are a range of policies, procedures and publications promoting inclusive practice. The publication *Raising Standards – Improving Outcomes Statutory Guidance: Early Years Outcomes Duty Childcare Act 2006* (HM Government 2008), for example, states: 'to improve the five Every Child Matters (ECM) outcomes of all young children (aged 0–5) in their area and reduce inequalities between them, through integrated early childhood services'. The 'Narrowing the Gap' agenda focuses on reducing the gap between the lowest achieving 20 per cent in the Early Years Foundation Stage and the rest, particularly children and families at risk of poor outcomes. Its importance is further emphasised in the *Early Years Self-Evaluation Form Guidance* (Ofsted 2009), when it asks 'How do we make sure all children irrespective of ethnicity, culture or religion, home language, family background, special educational needs and/or disabilities, gender or ability have the opportunity to experience a challenging and enjoyable programme of learning and development?'

EYFS settings are expected to identify the main disadvantaged groups in their community, namely those children and families at greatest risk of becoming excluded. Leaders need to be able to identify the groups and individuals, describe the interventions they have put in place, for example to 'reduce the gap', and most importantly, need to be able to support and challenge the team of practitioners to ensure that each child is able to progress as well as possible. In this case, the Leader as a Champion may not be the manager of the setting, but may instead have a different role, such as an Early Years Professional (EYP), Special Educational Needs Coordinator (SENCO) or Child Protection Officer (CPO). In the guidance to the EYP standards (CWDC, 2007), Standard 18 states that the EYP should 'Promote children's rights, equality, inclusion and anti-discriminatory practice in all aspects of their practice'. On assessment, candidates are judged on whether they:

- *ensure children's rights and entitlements are upheld*

- *treat all children fairly regardless of race, ethnicity, culture or religion, home language, family background, gender, or learning difficulties or disabilities*

- *make provision to include all children, using specialist services as needed*

- *lead and support colleagues to promote all children's rights, equality and inclusion.*

The Narrowing the Gap research undertaken by the National Foundation for Educational Research (NFER) found that 'the gap appears to be narrowed through leadership which emphasises six key ingredients', one of which is 'championing':

> *Championing the voice of vulnerable groups and encouraging their participation: establishing meaningful methods of consultation; having a genuine commitment to listen to service users and act on what they say ... Championing the needs of vulnerable groups through partnership working.*

> (Martin and others 2009, p. iv)

Championing the involvement of others

The majority of leaders ensure that others are involved in the development of their work, setting or project. The Leader as a Champion, however, sees the involvement of others as being at the heart of practice. Consultation is an ongoing process, not just when funding applications or evaluations are needed. All stakeholders are involved, from the very youngest children, who are well supported to make choices and offer opinions, to the most (and least) vocal parents and local councillors. The Leader as a Champion recognises the unique role and perspective that each of the stakeholders has, and the unique contribution each can make. Stakeholders include:

- children, parents, practitioners
- the wider community
- other professionals
- local, regional and national agencies
- the local authority.

(See Chapter 7 for more on consultation and Chapter 8 for more on involving a range of stakeholders in quality improvement initiatives.)

Championing quality

There are two leadership roles in the early years and playwork sector; the leader of the setting or organisation and the leader of practice (also described as leadership for learning). When considering the leader's responsibility to champion quality, we must consider the quality of services and processes for both the direct adult:child provision and also for the other aspects of the provision, for example, the processes for continuous professional development of the staff team or the service received by parents giving feedback.

The EYP standards state that the EYP should:

Be accountable for the delivery of high quality provision
                                    (Guidance to the Standards 2007, p. 3)

The delivery of high quality provision is the responsibility of more than just the EYP. Quality is the responsibility of everyone involved with the setting. It is expected that the EYP will be a 'quality champion' for children and families. The leader's role in this context is to 'fly the flag' for quality. This may be through being a role model, training, facilitating debate and discussion or supporting the undertaking of Quality Assurance (QA) as part of a Continuous Quality Improvement (CQI) agenda.

This is about saying that minimum standards are not 'good enough'. In the National Quality Improvement Network (NQIN) Principles, the former Children's Minister, Beverley Hughes said:

Every setting must strive to push the quality of its offer ever higher above Ofsted minimum standards.
                                    (Cooper and others 2007, p. 2)

Further discussion on quality can be found in Chapter 8. The following may offer some starting points:

- *Reflective practice:* How do you reflect on your practice, in terms of your leadership, your interaction with children, parents, colleagues and others? How do you encourage and support your team to engage in reflective practice? (See Chapter 2.)
- *Self-evaluation:* How do you self-evaluate your performance? How do you ensure that your teams engage in self-evaluation and that this is seen as an integral part of CQI? (See Chapter 8.)

- *Consultation:* How do you ensure that you and your team consult with the widest possible range of people? How do you consult with the very youngest children, the groups not yet engaged with as well as the most vocal individuals and organisations? (See Chapter 7.)
- *Quality of provision:* How do you ensure you are offering the best quality of provision? How do you use the above tools as part of your quality improvement strategy? (See Chapter 8.)

Supporting the leader to champion

Effective leaders have a range of resources, methods and strategies at their fingertips to support them in their work. Some of these will be tangible (such as documents), some will be ethical (such as strong beliefs and values) and some will be personal (skill, knowledge, qualities). Assess what is available to support you – what you have in place, what you need to develop and what else is available to support you in being a Leader as a Champion. The following highlights items for inclusion in your list of resources.

Reflection: activity

Your own 'champion's resources'

What do you know about the following points? How can they support you in your role? How can you use them in your role as a Leader as a Champion?

- key frameworks, policies and strategies
- research and reading
- training and development
- agencies and organisations
- reflective practice tools
- self-evaluation tools
- skills, knowledge and experience
- qualities and attitudes
- your personal support network.

How can you find out more about the above points?

Who can support you?

The case study below looks at an everyday occurrence where the opportunity arises to be a champion.

📖 Reflection: case study

Championing the rights of a range of stakeholders: Acorns Nursery

Acorns Nursery was well known within the local authority as a setting where children with a range of special educational needs and their families would be made welcome. The staff team were known for their dedication, enthusiasm and commitment in working with other professionals to achieve the best possible outcomes for children and their families.

It was a win–win situation as the practitioners gained a lot from working with a range of children and families. The knowledge and skills base of the practitioners grew, but so did their confidence in supporting all of the children's individual needs. Other benefits to the organisation included the team's increased ability and confidence to work together to overcome barriers to inclusion and to support each other. Practitioners were keen to continue learning to improve their practice and the organisation was very happy to enable the team to access training, visit other settings and try out new ideas.

The result of this growing reputation was that whilst the nursery was already supporting a significant number of children with a wide variety of additional needs, many of whom needed one-on-one support, they were being inundated with additional requests. Supporting and caring for such a diverse group of children was extremely rewarding but could also be particularly exhausting, both emotionally and physically. The nursery manager was aware of the benefits to the organisation, but was also aware of the financial costs, as additional funding was not provided for enhanced staffing levels.

The 'Tipping Point' (Gladwell 2000) for the nursery came when an existing customer, the parent of an autistic child, comfortable with the way her child had settled, explained that she now felt able to return to full-time work. The parent asked to increase her child's hours from two sessions a week in term-time to full-time (8am to 6pm), 51 weeks per year.

The manager was faced with a dilemma – how could she simultaneously champion the rights of the parent, the child, the staff team and the organisation? How could she act in a way that reflected her commitment to inclusion but also respect the needs of her team?

The nursery manager approached another local provider with whom Acorns had previously worked collaboratively. Between the two providers they arranged to offer the full-time place required by the parent, to share the additional staffing costs, and to work collaboratively and learn from each other. The child had a key person in each setting, which although not the ideal choice, meant that each key person was emotionally and physically able to give 100 per cent whenever the child attended. The two settings, and the two practitioners, were also able to access training together and even share staffing at times so that support for the child was not disrupted.

Think of the case study from the point of view of the different stakeholders; the leader, the practitioners, the other setting, the parent and the child. You could use either a SWOT analysis approach (assessing the strengths, weaknesses, opportunities and threats) or use the 'Six Thinking Hats' approach described in Chapter 3.

Questions:

- How would you have dealt with this situation?

- How would you champion inclusion?

- How would you champion involving others?

- How would you champion quality practice?

Behaving with integrity and making positive choices

The Leader as a Champion sounds idealistic when talking about values and principles, but being a champion means living and acting according to those values and principles. This section looks at some of the dilemmas that a person might face, particularly when championing the rights of vulnerable people.

Reflection: case study

Workplace bullying is illegal and there are procedures in place to tackle this. Sadly, people still find themselves in difficult situations, such as the one described below. Leaders need to ensure that staff are treated with respect and dignity at all times. Read the scenario below, and then reflect on the questions: how do you ensure that this kind of behaviour does not happen within your organisation, at any level?

Favouritism

Karen worked in a large staff team. The manager of the setting often abused her power as a manager and was well known for favouring her 'special friends' amongst the team.

The rest of the team knew that the manager would pick fault with members of staff indiscriminately and the manager was well known for humiliating staff in front of peers and parents.

None of the staff team stood up for themselves or others when these situations occurred, but accepted it as 'their turn' and recognised that they were being 'picked on'.

Questions:

- How do you ensure staff are treated equally?
- How do you ensure staff are treated respectfully?
- How do you ensure staff have opportunity to voice their opinions?
- How do you challenge staff appropriately?

As adults, we can make decisions about whether we are going to accept situations like the one above or do something about them. We may not be able to stand up to an abusive leader for fear of retribution and repercussion. Even in situations where fear of financial or job loss is the case, as adults we have choices in how we deal with conflict. The five options available are:

1. do nothing
2. change the situation
3. change yourself
4. try to change the other person's behaviour
5. leave.

Sometimes, like Karen, we recognise that neither confrontation nor continuing to work in the same organisation is an option, as the other person's behaviour is unlikely to change.

When reflecting on this, think about the amount of choice each individual has. Some people appear to have more choice than others. They may be able to afford to leave a job they do not enjoy because of their financial situation. They may feel more able to apply for and gain new employment because of qualifications, experience or a good interview technique. Or they may feel better able to explain to the manager how they feel when treated in this way because of good interpersonal communication skills.

Similarly, there may be many reasons why people do not challenge poor behaviour, for example, lack of self-esteem, lack of knowledge that there could be another way, or the fear of restricted career opportunities. There is no simple answer to a situation like this. What proves effective in one situation may not be the case in another. We have a right to stand up for ourselves if we feel we are being treated inappropriately. However, the situation becomes less clear when we start defending the rights of our colleagues – we could just make a situation that they find tolerable even worse.

In cases such as Karen's, how can you make positive choices? The answer could be to look at your options and commit to your decision. This way you are much less likely to become the victim of stress or regret, both of which will affect your well-being. If you decide to stay, you know why you are doing so, and can remind yourself of the reasons and stay with dignity. If you decide to try and change the situation, it could be through actions rather than words. And, though not the perfect choice, there is the option of 'doing nothing', at least for the time being. The psychology of making a choice of 'doing nothing' could in fact help you cope with the situation: this way you have made the choice, rather than having it forced upon you.

Sometimes we are placed in a position where we are presented with difficult choices. We may not have a leadership role, but we may be given the opportunity to stand up for the rights of others who are not able to do so themselves. This might mean challenging the views or actions of those in authority within your organisation, perhaps of a valued customer, or perhaps someone in a regulatory or inspection role.

Reflection: case study

Championing children's rights

Daniel started working at a full daycare nursery. He had been on placement in two other settings but this was his first paid employment after leaving university and gaining his EYP status. He was keen to learn about his new workplace and make a good impression on his colleagues.

On his first day, Daniel was asked to cover lunch in the baby room. When he went to pick up Adam, a five-month-old baby who was strapped into a baby bouncer and who was obviously distressed and crying loudly, the room leader told Daniel not to. The room leader said that Adam just cried for attention. She went on to say that if Daniel picked Adam up it would encourage him to cry for attention all the more and that would make life very difficult for the staff team, who had lots of jobs to get done throughout the day. She then warned Daniel that it was not a good idea to let children get too attached as it sometimes upset the parents and made things difficult when moving between rooms.

In this situation, Daniel needs to display leadership. It could be argued that he is morally obliged to champion the rights of the child. There may be many reasons why he might feel awkward in doing so, but there are ways of doing it that might not jeopardise his relationships with his new colleagues. If Daniel is to retain his integrity, he has no choice but to share his understanding of babies' and young children's needs and development.

Questions:

- How could Daniel share his understanding of young babies appropriately?
- How could Daniel 'lead' in this situation?
- How could Daniel champion children's rights?

Place yourself in the above situation:

- As a practitioner, how would you deal with this situation?
- As a leader, how would you deal with this situation?

Are your answers to these two questions different, and if so – why?

When you are faced with a difficult situation be true to your personal values and behave with integrity. (For further discussion on conflict, see Chapter 7.) Leadership is demonstrated in the way you behave with others. This is at the heart of the Leader as a Champion:

> But in the long run, people will trust and respect you if you are honest and open and kind with them. You care enough to confront. And to be trusted, it is said, is greater than to be loved.

(Covey 1992, p. 197)

Chapter summary

Integrity, honesty, passion and persistence are key components of leadership. Leaders stand up for a cause and for what is right, and act in a principled way. They are not afraid to challenge.

Leaders champion inclusion and ensure everyone has a voice, and that it is heard. In the early years and playwork sector, they identify disadvantaged groups and strive to 'Narrow the Gap' between them and the rest. They work with others to ensure that all children achieve the best possible outcomes.

A culture of continuous quality improvement is nurtured within the organisation, aiming to deliver services of ever higher quality.

Leaders draw on a range of resources, skills, knowledge and personal qualities in order to champion a cause. They support others in developing and sharing a collective vision.

6 The Leader as a Motivator

*The most important motive for work in school and in life is ...
pleasure in work, pleasure in its result, and the knowledge
of the value of the result – to the community.*

(Albert Einstein)

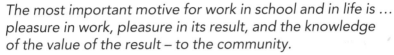

The Leader as a Motivator

Effective leaders care for others. They understand the importance of emotionally
intelligent relationships and place value on creating positive working environments in
which practitioners feel fulfilled.

We are all familiar with the analogy of the carrot and stick as
alternative ways of motivating a stubborn mule to move forward; the
carrot as the reward and the stick as punishment. Transactional
leaders (see Chapter 1) favour this approach when motivating their
staff. But how effective is it as a method of getting a job done well,
of encouraging great teamwork and encouraging people to think for
themselves, reflect on their work and suggest or make
improvements? This chapter explores the role of the leader in
motivating the staff team, not by providing a reward and sanction
regime, but by considering their needs and interests.

Why do you go to work every day? This might seem a strange
question to ask, but have you ever thought about why you actually
work in the profession you do? We are all motivated by different
things. Some of us work with children and families because we want
to make a difference, some of us because we fell into the job and
some of us simply because we need to pay the bills every month.
Having said that, the pay we receive for the roles we do is not always

the prime motivator, it very often is not the main reason for going to work. Think of the parents you work with, who return to their jobs with the support of your setting in providing childcare. Parents often say that by the time they have paid for travel to and from work, childcare and the additional costs associated with work such as lunches, there is very little salary left over, thus it follows that they too are probably motivated by something other than money.

Reflection: activity

Why do people go to work?

Do a straw poll of the people you know – friends and family, rather than work colleagues.

Ask them why they do the jobs they do. You will be surprised at some of the answers.

Note: You may want to think about whether you ask work colleagues. They may feel uncomfortable answering this type of question from you as a peer/leader or may just give you those answers they think you want to hear.

The reasons we go to work every day are decided, on the whole, by our motivations: what motivates us to do a particular job or task and why. Abraham Maslow, a key writer on motivation, developed his Hierarchy of Needs in 1954. Maslow's theory is simple: the triangle in the diagram of the Hierarchy of Needs represents the requirements of human life. Maslow discussed how there are five stages to developing motivation, based on needs being met.

Maslow's Hierarchy of Needs

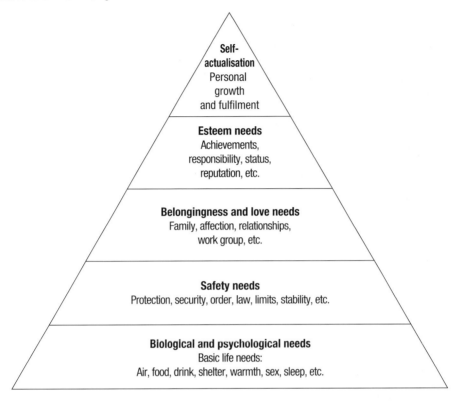

Reproduced with permission from Maslow, A (1970) *Motivation and Personality*. 2nd ed.
New York: Harper and Row.

Maslow's theory is well respected and easy to understand: if the basic human needs are in jeopardy or threatened in some way, how can we move upwards towards being fulfilled? If you are worried about your health, you will not be able to function at your usual level and there will be a dip in your commitment or ability to work. Likewise, the person worried about the roof over their head (either due to holes and leaks or due to monetary worries) will not be able to think creatively. Being aware of Maslow's theory and being aware of the situations your team and colleagues find themselves in can be incredibly useful to the Leader as a Motivator.

As well as the motivation to go to work every day, we are also motivated by different things in terms of the tasks we undertake. For example, think of all the tasks you undertake on a daily, weekly or monthly basis. There will be some tasks you thoroughly enjoy doing and others that you put off until the very last minute. Do you know why you like some tasks more than others?

! Reflection: activity

Motivation to complete tasks

Task	Motivation	Motivation rating
Filling in local authority returns	Linked to funding	5 (high)
Completing sickness records	Have to be done	1 (low)

Use the grid example above for every task you undertake. Then rate your personal motivation for completing that task: 5 being high motivation, 1 being low motivation.

Some examples have been given to get you going.

It should be possible for you to see what motivates you, how you are motivated and what fails to motivate. Then reflect on your team and colleagues. You will know that some team members complete some tasks quickly and with obvious enjoyment, whereas other tasks will need constant reminders and chasing from you. How can you find out what tasks people enjoy doing and which they avoid? And how can this help in your role as a leader? Bear in mind the ideas discussed in the motivation and de-motivation sections in Chapter 3.

Once you know what motivates your team and colleagues to come to work every day and you know which tasks they are motivated to do efficiently and with enjoyment, it should then be much easier to allocate job roles and tasks. For example, if you have a team member who worries about their 'safety needs' (fear of the unknown or the importance of routine) you may find it unhelpful to ask them to lead on a major change within the setting. Similarly, if you have a team member who is new and needs to feel part of the team, you could allocate tasks that encourage their social needs to be met.

Motivation to learn

We go to work for a variety of reasons, and one may be to learn new skills. For example, we learn from colleagues, from attending training, from information at team meetings or from access to new research and documentation. There are some skills we learn quicker than others, and some that require a great deal of personal motivation for us to conquer.

Gagné (1985), in his discussion of the conditions of learning, lists his first item as 'to motivate individuals to learn'.

1. Gain their attention and motivate them
2. Tell the learner of expected outcomes
3. Stimulate recall of relevant knowledge and experience and recognition of relevant skills and emotions
4. Present new stimuli relating to the learner and the task: develop new opportunities
5. Activate the learner's response
6. Provide learning guidance
7. Provide speedy feedback
8. Appraise performance (offer extended feedback)
9. Provide for transferability
10. Ensure retention (and encourage practice)

Gagne's list can be used to evaluate the effectiveness of teaching and learning in a traditional teaching environment, for example, the classroom. Considering the list in terms of learning within our job roles, including, but not exclusively, training, the first two points have a much wider meaning than just getting people to physically 'sit up and take notice'. 'Gaining their attention', 'motivation' and 'understanding expected outcomes' relate directly to the leader's role to help others understand the issues and possible solutions (see Chapter 3) and to developing and sharing the organisation's vision (see Chapter 5).

Using Gagné's conditions of learning as a top ten list for motivation to learn, how will you, as a leader, ensure that individuals within your team:

- are motivated to learn: how do you gain their attention?
- understand what they are expected to learn/do as a result and why?
- are supported to use their knowledge, experience and skills?
- have opportunities to try new knowledge, skills or understanding, etc.?
- are motivated to be involved?
- have appropriate support, encouragement and advice?
- receive appropriate and timely feedback?
- understand their learning, and have opportunity for review and reflection (for themselves and from others)?
- have the opportunity to test new learning in a variety of contexts?
- remember and practise new skills, knowledge, etc.?

Chapter 2 offers further support to encourage learning. In terms of motivation, you can find out what the teams and individuals within your organisation are interested in and then look at how you can develop knowledge and learning in those areas.

Interest is a motivation to learn at depth and the satisfaction gained will be a positive reinforcer for more learning behaviour of that type.

(Moon 1999, p. 32)

If we are interested in a subject, that interest will motivate us to learn more and to continue to develop that interest. For example, an individual is particularly interested in working with parents and asks to attend a training course on partnership with parents. When the parents' notice board needs to be developed, however, it is the person who always does displays who is asked yet again, while the person interested in working with parents watches wistfully from the sidelines. In a busy work environment our interests can sometimes get overlooked, and individual motivation easily lost.

We have discussed motivation to learn. The chances are that you and other members of your team are undertaking further training and qualifications. These opportunities can be a source of pleasure and fulfilment or, equally, a source of stress. It is likely that we access formal training either because we want to, we feel we ought to or because someone says we have to.

We have all attended training that we have enjoyed, learnt from and been inspired by. Chances are that we wanted to be there. The flip side of this is how we feel about training we did not choose to attend.

Reflection: case study

Influences on personal motivation

Bilal was attending a module on developing facilitation skills as part of his degree. He had not had the opportunity as a young man to attend university, so, as a mature student, was relishing what he saw as a second chance. Bilal attended the first session with a high degree of personal motivation, a readiness to learn and a willingness to become involved. He therefore felt happy at the prospect of this new module.

Halfway through the first session, Bilal found his attention wavering, not due to lack of interest on his part, but due to an apparent lack of interest among some of the other students. Some whispered amongst themselves, one read a newspaper, one ate throughout the session and another was asleep with her head on the desk. At break time Bilal mentioned this to the tutor. The tutor explained that this happened every year. Some of the other students were forced to attend the first session of the module as part of their degrees in other professions.

It is easy to see why Bilal finds his attention wavering and have some sympathy for his situation. But how might the other students feel? How do you feel when forced to do something that is of no interest to you?

Think about how you feel about the training you attend depending on whether it is being undertaken because you want to or because someone says you have to.

Questions:

- Who instigated the training – did you decide to do it?

- Why are you undertaking the learning – if it was suggested to you, do you know why?

- When and where is it happening?

- How do you feel about it?

- What are you personally gaining from it? Is it challenging you enough? Is it too challenging?

- Do you know how it will benefit your organisation and its improvement priorities?

- What will you do as a result of the training? Will or can anything change?

Reflection: activity

Your motivation to undertake tasks

Consider the above questions for tasks you undertake within your work life; for example, how you feel when the tasks are forced upon you or hold no interest for you.

Think about your team and how they feel when undertaking routine tasks within their roles and also additional tasks that they, you or others have identified for them. As leader, are you aware of how they feel? How do you, or could you, find out?

Influences on team motivation and team morale

We have looked at the possible reasons why people in your team come to work every day. As leader, you need to know what your team like about the work environment and what they find difficult or would want to change. For example, you have to provide opportunities to access training and professional development and also opportunities to be able to socialise and get to know each other. Remembering birthdays and making people feel included and part of the team are important skills to cultivate. You should encourage people to manage their work/life balance, for example, by supporting time off to attend their children's school plays and open days or taking a shared responsibility for booking annual leave. You need to know what makes your team happy and fulfilled in their roles.

Chapter 3 discussed Ferre Laevers' theory of well-being and involvement as being crucial indicators of a child's ability to access deep level learning and compared this to adult well-being and fulfilment in the workplace. Just as children need learning opportunities that stretch and challenge them without being too difficult (see Vygotsky's 'zone of proximal development', 1978), adults also need to have challenging opportunities. Success and achievement can be hugely motivating, even when someone has had to hold your hand the first time you tried something.

For every occasion you can think of where you or a colleague felt great satisfaction at having achieved something perceived as difficult, you will probably also be able to think of someone who has not wanted to be challenged or pushed out of their comfort zone. Nevertheless, it is equally important to offer challenging opportunities to such people. Sometimes leaders need to provoke the 'chaos' or the 'edge of chaos' where learning and innovation happens (Gleick 1987).

Returning to Maslow's Hierarchy of Needs (p. 87), at the foot of the pyramid are the basic human needs – sleep, food, drink, and so on – without which we cannot survive. This is the widest part of the triangle as it is the foundation on which human life depends. Maslow's theory is that once the basic needs are met, we can move up the sections in the pyramid towards self-actualisation. We can then progress towards higher learning, feel secure in taking risks and try out new ideas. It would not be sensible to push the person whose base of the triangle was unstable. People whose foundations are firm can be, and might welcome opportunities to develop their 'needs' of belonging and respect. This in turn offers the individual and the team opportunities to take risks and try ideas in an environment of mutual support.

Offering opportunity and motivating individuals enables the move up the pyramid. As individuals climb higher, their self-esteem increases, their confidence improves and they look for approval and respect from others. The Leader as a Motivator needs to be aware of when people are ready for new challenges, and be prepared to act accordingly.

When individuals are at this stage, no matter how supportive you are, or how many opportunities you offer, they begin to contemplate career changes and promotion. This could be a time when practitioners want to develop their own self-esteem – they believe they can do better, and want more responsibility. It could also be a time of wanting a greater challenge than that currently offered, leading towards fulfilment and personal growth. A denial of these needs will lead to frustration. And frustration is one of the biggest causes of de-motivation, as discussed in Chapter 3.

Reflection: case studies

Motivation in a new role – case study A

Tarija had completed initial training, kept up with professional development issues and through quiet determination had worked her way up the career ladder within the organisation. After a while Tarija realised that further progression was going to be difficult because the people in senior roles seemed happy and unlikely to move on to other things. Tarija began to look elsewhere and was delighted when she was successful in gaining promotion within another large organisation.

After her first week in the role, Tarija's new manager, Marion, explained that she would like a catch-up meeting every Monday morning at 8.30am. The purpose of the meeting would be to discuss any issues from the previous week and consider work for the current week. Tarija felt this would be useful, as being new to the role and not based in the same office as Marion, it would be practical to have weekly support meetings.

Within three months it became apparent that the meetings held different purposes for Tarija and Marion. Each week Marion would ask for progress reports and then follow up in writing to people whom Tarija had met the previous week. Spending associated with the large budget attached to the project could only be authorised by Marion, so even small things such as paperclips and office supplies had to be asked for, scrutinised and agreed upon. Tarija began to dread the Monday morning meetings and found that it affected her weekends; she suffered from a growing sense of nausea as the working week grew closer and an inability to sleep on Sunday nights.

At one of their Monday morning meetings, Tarija mentioned that she had been invited to a meeting to discuss a forthcoming project. Marion decided that it should be her, as manager, that attended and not Tarija. After considering this for a moment, Tarija suggested they attend the meeting together. Marion deliberated for a while but eventually agreed. At the meeting Marion publicly disagreed with Tarija on several points. At one point she shouted across the room, 'How do you know? You're too new to this.'

When Tarija returned to her office, Cathy, the administrator, commented that Tarija looked upset and asked if everything was OK. Tarija did not want to discuss the situation with Cathy as she was unsure where Cathy's loyalties lay. To avoid further discussion, Tarija said she was just a little tired.

Questions:

- How do you think Tarija feels?

- How do you think Marion feels?

- What issues do you think might arise? And why?

- How could the above situation have been avoided?

Motivation in a new role – case study B

Roisin had completed initial training, kept up with professional development issues and through quiet determination had worked her way up the career ladder within the organisation. After a while Roisin realised that further progression was going to be difficult because the people in senior roles seemed happy and unlikely to move on to other things. Roisin began to look elsewhere and was delighted when she was successful in gaining promotion within another large organisation.

After her first week in the role, Roisin's new manager, Donald, explained that he would like a catch-up meeting every Monday morning at 8.30am. The purpose of the meeting would be to discuss any issues from the previous week and consider work for the current week. Roisin felt this would be useful, as being new to the role and not based in the same office as Donald, it would be practical to have weekly support meetings.

The meetings progressed well. Every week Donald would ask for progress reports and would always offer praise where he felt Roisin had performed well. If Roisin asked for help, Donald would offer suggestions on how to move projects forward, on who else within the organisation might be able to help, or ask if she wanted him to attend meetings to support her.

At one of their Monday morning meetings, Roisin mentioned that she had been invited to a governor's meeting at a local school to discuss a forthcoming project. Donald asked about the new project, and Roisin admitted to feeling a little nervous about speaking to a large group of governors. Donald asked if Roisin would like his support at the meeting, and so it was agreed that they would attend together.

At the governor's meeting, Roisin began by asking questions about how she could help with the new project that the governors of the school were hoping to establish. At one point, a question was asked directly of Donald, he explained briefly what his organisation could do to support the school, but then passed the question on to Roisin, saying, 'Really you need to speak to Roisin, this is her area. Roisin, why don't you tell the governors about the project you led on at Summertown School? It was a very successful project and in essence very similar to this one.'

When Roisin returned to her office, Leah, the administrator, commented that Roisin looked less nervous than before the governor's meeting and asked how the meeting had gone.

Questions:

- How do you think Roisin feels?

- How do you think Donald feels?

- How do you think this will improve Roisin's motivation? Why?

The first case study alerts us to the very real danger of de-motivating staff by not being sensitive to their needs and feelings: a new and enthusiastic team member is too closely managed by an over-enthusiastic or over-controlling line manager. Also, as this is a new role for Tarija, chances are that there may not be a support network of trusted colleagues whom Tarija could talk to in confidence. If Tarija continued in this role, it might have an impact on her motivation, self-esteem and confidence. Suppose then that something happened to threaten Tarija's physiological needs, we can see how quickly the situation could degenerate and cause serious damage to Tarija's well-being.

The second case study shows how supportive leadership can encourage and empower individuals. Donald's supportive style during the weekly meetings allowed Roisin to ask for help when she needed it. Likewise, when answering the question asked directly of him at the governor's meeting, Donald passed the leadership of the project back to Roisin, at the same time as subtly helping Roisin discuss work in a similar area where she had previously been successful. As this is a new role for Roisin, think about how she feels to be able to speak openly and honestly to her manager, and ask for help and feel supported when unsure. Suppose something were to happen to threaten Roisin's physiological needs, how might Roisin feel in undertaking her daily role? What do you think would happen to her motivation, self-esteem and confidence? Now compare this to your thoughts on Tarija above.

A final thought about motivation: Transformational Leaders (see Chapter 1) care for their teams and support individuals to achieve more than they thought possible. In contrast, Transactional Leaders use the carrot and stick method to get the job done. Being treating as a robot rather than as a person with thoughts and opinions, needs and emotions, could leave you feeling resentful and undervalued. As discussed previously, leaders need to seek to understand their teams; their interests and motivations, their strengths and weaknesses. Leadership is about relationships. Rather than thinking about team as cogs within the organisational machine, it is useful to think of the organisation as a web of interconnecting relationships.

Chapter summary

Leaders need to understand what motivates people to go to work, to learn and to undertake tasks.

Well-being is crucial for adults, just as it is for children. Adults will work (and learn) more effectively if their needs and interests are met. There are certain fundamental needs that, if not met, threaten our ability to function properly (Maslow 1970).

Leaders need to challenge staff appropriately in order to stimulate and motivate them. Sometimes leaders need to support staff to take risks and make changes that may initially challenge their well-being.

Motivation methods may vary – leaders using a transactional approach use the carrot and stick method, while leaders using a transformational approach seek to instigate change in people to achieve more than they thought possible.

7 The Leader as a Problem Solver

Go to the people. Learn from them. Live with them. Start with what they know. Build with what they have. The best of leaders when the job is done, when the task is accomplished … the people will say we have done it ourselves.

(Lao Tzu)

The Leader as a Problem Solver

The Leader as a Problem Solver knows that prevention is better than cure. The best way to manage problems is to have processes in place to avoid them being created in the first place. When problems do occur, leaders need to have a range of strategies to assist them and endeavour to learn from the situation. Leaders should not work in isolation but need to develop strong supportive teams that are capable of identifying and solving problems themselves.

This chapter looks at how organisations seek and receive feedback on their performance, particularly in terms of compliments, complaints and concerns, and how this can be used to improve quality. It also looks at how leaders can give effective feedback, focusing on the difficult conversations that are to be had, for example, during capability and disciplinary procedures. Teamwork and building effective teams are considered as ways of not only avoiding problems, but also of identifying and solving problems. This chapter also looks at some of the difficult things a leader has to deal with and how leaders can develop a range of strategies for understanding, unravelling and sorting difficult, knotty or complex situations.

In previous chapters, we looked at how the improving of qualities, skills and knowledge could help you develop your leadership. For example, you might decide to use mentoring skills to support your team, ideas from Chapter 3 to support risk taking and reflection, or develop an emotionally intelligent workplace to support motivation. These ideas come with a wealth of references to direct you to other sources of support along your journey towards leadership.

Being a leader is not always easy. When things are going well it is usually because of 'great teamwork'. When things are going badly it is usually the leader who is blamed and to whom everyone looks to for the solution. The leader has the stewardship of the organisation's health and well-being. This includes the business, the employees and the customers, the most important of whom are the children and families the services are meant for. The leader is often responsible for regulation and inspection, and in terms of legal requirements it is usually the leader who takes ultimate responsibility.

There is now an expectation that leaders support and challenge their organisations to achieve Continuous Quality Improvement (CQI). For the Leader as a Problem Solver, this means being aware of the areas of weakness in the organisation. It also means the leader encouraging a culture of innovation; and requires that staff be willing to take risks and try things out in order to find new ways of working. Problems can be seen as challenges and learning opportunities – we can learn from our own and other people's mistakes.

Anyone can hold the helm when the sea is calm.

Syrus (First century BC Latin writer)

Meeting stakeholder expectations: compliments, complaints and consultation

We are encouraged to think of mistakes and complaints as learning opportunities. This is important, but we must also solve the problem or deal with the complaint. It is not only what we do, but how we do it that makes a difference to the outcome. It may be worth thinking about who you believe your customers or stakeholders are. Parents are likely to be at the top of your customer list, but does it also include outside agencies? And where, for example, do children feature as customers?

How do you view complaints?

We are expected to record complaints as part of our statutory duties (DCSF 2008). The majority of complaints that are recorded for Ofsted purposes are official written complaints from parents. But how do you view verbal 'complaints' or even 'little niggles' – for example, the parent who comments: 'I don't want you to think I'm complaining, and Annabel is very happy here, but I just needed to ask you …'. What do you do with these comments from parents? How do you share them with the team and encourage the team to share them with you?

If a customer is unhappy with an aspect of your service they may do one of the following things:

1. say nothing
2. tell other people
3. tell you if you ask
4. tell you without being prompted.

Customers are much more likely to tell others of poor service than go with the first option. You will want to avoid this as you would like the opportunity to discuss the issue and hopefully put things right: after all, word of mouth is a valuable marketing tool. In options three and four, the customer lets you know that they are unhappy with your service. When and how (written and verbal) do you approach customers to ask them what they think? Similarly, when and how do you provide opportunities (written and verbal) for customers to approach you with their thoughts about your service? The aim should be to retain customers and for them to give other people positive information about the service you offer.

How do your customers know they are being listened to or that you will listen?

This is not about tricks you can employ to demonstrate you are listening. If you have ever been professionally listened to by someone who is not really trying to understand where you are coming from, you will know how insulting and inauthentic that feels. This is about genuinely caring for what the other person has to say. You may do some of the same things as the professional listener, for example, maintaining eye contact and checking for meaning with regard to what the other person has said, but the difference lies in the attitude of the listener – a true listener is one who is listening to really understand the other person's point of view. As a leader, you can role model being a genuine listener.

If the feedback came in written form, or was passed on to you from another practitioner, you need to make sure that the customer is aware that you have received the feedback and that you are going to do something about it, even if this is no more than having a conversation with the complainant.

But what about those people who have a concern, but from past experience (perhaps nothing to do with you) do not think it is worth letting you know? One way to let them know that you do listen is to put this into practice and demonstrate your willingness to listen. For example, you could include notes in your newsletters or on the parents' notice board: 'Several parents in the Blue Room have commented on the lack of fresh fruit and vegetables on the menu. We have therefore …' or, 'In response to parental concern about children playing out in all weathers, we have purchased waterproof coats, umbrellas and a number of spare sets of Wellingtons'.

This may encourage parents who have not previously offered feedback and suggestions to begin doing so. Teams who see genuine care for customers will be encouraged to behave in the same way and will hopefully understand, that they, the team, matter too.

How do you deal with complaints?

How you view complaints and how you receive and deal with them will have an impact on how your team deals with complaints. The Leader as a Problem Solver looks to understand the issue and how the same or similar scenarios can be avoided in future. Even better, such a leader attempts to find out how the situation could be improved so that the quality of service is not just acceptable, but excellent.

Reflection: case study

Dealing with complaints

Marty is the manager of a childcare setting. There are 10 members of staff, including a cook, a cleaner and a caretaker. A parent approaches Marty and casually mentions that her two-and-a-half-year-old daughter had used a swear word. When the parent asked the child where she had heard such a word, the child said, 'lady at play school'. The parent had been unable to find out which 'lady at play school' had used the word.

Marty calls an emergency staff meeting for later that day, after the children have left. All members of the team are expected to attend and one member of the team is instructed to return to the setting after attending a training course.

Marty explains to the team about the complaint from the parent and demands to know who had used the swear word in the child's presence. The team all deny knowledge of using such a word and Marty is visibly angry: 'I am appalled that none of you have the bottle to open up. I can't have parents complaining: I have the business to think of. I need to reassure the parents that I have identified the person responsible. I expect the culprit to be in my office first thing tomorrow morning, to own up and apologise to the parent and we can discuss consequences later.'

Questions:

- How do you think the staff team feel?

- How do you think Marty feels?

- Why do you think Marty has behaved in this way?

- How would you handle the above situation?

This is an extreme example, but the key message here is: leaders who conduct 'witch hunts' to find out 'who did it' and therefore create a 'blame culture' will not encourage teams to listen to, and pass on customer feedback.

It is also worth bearing in mind that the size of the complaint or feedback is not important. Leaders who only take notice of the big complaints (perhaps the ones they have to report) are missing opportunities to make improvements and show customers that their opinions matter. Likewise, positive feedback comments, no matter how small, should always be passed on to the relevant team or individual.

Consultation and feedback from other stakeholders

It is an expectation of the Ofsted Self-Evaluation that you capture the views of parents and children and say how you have made improvements in response to their suggestions. This idea sits well with the frequently used definition of quality, 'meeting the customer requirements' (Oakland 2003, p. 5) or, in the case of public sector and not-for-profit organisations, 'meeting the requirements and expectations of service users and other stakeholders whilst keeping costs to a minimum' (Moullin 2002, p. 15). (For more on definitions of quality, see Chapter 8). It sounds simple, but if you want to meet the needs of all your stakeholders, you need to know what those needs are. How do you know what is important to your main stakeholder groups, such as funders, your employees and the children and families you provide services for? How do you check to find out if their needs are being met?

Consultation has become a buzzword in recent years, particularly in relation to consultation with children. However, it is not always easy to ask children or adults what their needs are and what is important to them. It is very easy to say, 'Yes, we consult ... We have a comments box, and we ask the children what new toys we should buy.' This could be the beginnings of consultation, or could merely be paying lip service to consultation.

Think about consultations in which you have been involved, maybe for local planning developments in your area, or when you have responded to a consultation about new guidance or good practice. How did you feel when the results came out? Had your views been listened to or did you feel as if the decisions had been made regardless of the consultation? Consider the stakeholders you work with. How do they feel about the consultations you undertake? Do they feel the decisions have already been made or do they feel you have listened to them – and how would you know?

Helping staff to meet expectations: supporting good performance and practice

The Leader as a Problem Solver knows that prevention is better than cure. If you know what is expected of you then you are far more likely to meet or exceed expectations, or negotiate different expectations, thus avoiding problems in the first place.

In the same way that we establish with external stakeholders, for example, parents, what they expect from us and what we can be reasonably expected to provide in terms of service, leaders also need to establish two-way expectations with employees. Procedures such as induction, supervision and appraisals, and documentation such as staff handbooks, job descriptions and contracts help to bring focus to this process.

Feedback as a means of improving understanding and learning

Ongoing and continuing opportunities to discuss performance and practice, such as formal supervision and appraisal processes, and informal opportunities such as open door policies, help keep people on the right track and can be very motivating, if handled correctly. It is important that supervision and appraisal systems are seen as an integral part of quality improvement; as supportive procedures, rather than simply as ways of addressing problems and issues. It would be unfair and unprofessional to leave serious performance issues until an annual appraisal or review. When performance is not up to expectation, it is important that it be confronted sooner rather than later.

It is vital to ensure, particularly in multi-disciplinary teams, that everyone has a shared understanding of the words used. For example, 'supervision' in terms of social work means having a person with whom to discuss case loads in a supportive, almost mentor-like way. To others, supervision could mean getting your time sheet signed. Each individual's understanding of particular words will depend on their previous experience of leadership style and the language used in other areas of the play, learning and care fields. Differences in understanding words and terminology used can cause problems and this is an area where the Leader as a Problem Solver should strive to develop a shared understanding within the team.

For many people, giving and receiving feedback is linked to emotions and can cause extremes of emotional response. If we like the feedback, it makes us happy; if we do not like the feedback, it makes us unhappy. Giving positive feedback is often seen as easier than giving negative feedback. There is, however, a different way of looking at it. The following quote is taken from the Leeds Metropolitan University (LMU) Professional Diploma in Mentoring, and offers an alternative view of feedback:

> *... feedback is neither positive nor negative: it is the opinion of one person to another, to increase understanding.*
>
> (Tarbitt 2005, bk 2, p. 97)

The above definition of feedback is appropriate to the early years and playwork sector and is also in keeping with the way in which feedback and encouragement is offered to children. It has been suggested that the word 'learning' be added to the LMU definition:

> *... feedback is neither positive nor negative: it is the opinion of one person to another, to increase understanding or learning.*

By encouraging the team to adopt this definition, the Leader as a Problem Solver will find the giving of feedback easier and will also find that the person receiving it is less likely to have extreme emotional responses. That is not to say that as leaders we should no longer offer praise or encouragement or pass on words of thanks and gratitude to our teams, nor indeed that we should ignore performance-related issues: it should all be given and received in an ethos of developing understanding and learning. This definition could be discussed openly and honestly at a team meeting, with explanations, debate and discussion around what constitutes 'feedback', 'learning' and 'understanding'. In this way, the team are enabled to have ownership of feedback throughout the setting and to reach a shared understanding.

Reflection: activity

In these two case studies, two teams have very different experiences of receiving feedback:

Feedback

Team A
Feedback is usually only given when something goes wrong, or there is a complaint. The leader occasionally remembers to pass on positive comments from parents and other stakeholders.

The leader brings to a team meeting the decision to introduce peer observation.

Team B
The team have adopted the LMU definition of feedback. The leader brings to a team meeting the decision to introduce peer observation.

Questions:

- How do Team A feel about feedback?
- How does the leader of Team A feel about feedback?
- How do you think Team A will feel about the introduction of peer observation?

- How do Team B feel about feedback?
- How does the leader of Team B feel about feedback?
- How do you think Team B will feel about the introduction of peer observation?

- Which team would you prefer to work in?
- Which team would you prefer to lead?

If we accept the LMU quote regarding feedback, it becomes an understood part of improving practice (regardless of who is giving the feedback). It does not come as a shock when there are difficulties to discuss and should decrease the incidence of defensiveness and upset. People ought to have timely and ongoing feedback, which should include:

- a clear explanation or demonstration of what is expected
- any improvement that is required together with a timescale for this
- praise and recognition of improvements made
- encouragement for further understanding and learning
- the opportunity for the individual to offer ideas
- where they can look to for ongoing support.

If, as leaders, we are using feedback mechanisms to deal with performance issues, it is vital that we have the information we need, which may include:

- job description, policies and procedures
- evidence regarding the lack of performance (dates of continuous lateness and so on)
- evidence of improvements
- a way of recording the discussion, outcomes and timescales

- support mechanisms for the individual (for example, the training available, external support and details of any support offered by the organisation).

It is important that the member of staff concerned has copies of the above, plus minutes of any meetings that are held. This way they have the paperwork to refer to and can begin to monitor their own progress.

Capability, disciplinary and 'organisational culture' issues

An organisation has a variety of means for letting employees know what is expected of them, for example, contracts of employment, job descriptions, policies and procedures, and vision statements. These are all explicit (clear and obvious) expectations. Within any organisation there are also implicit expectations: rules that are unwritten, unspoken, but generally understood by most people. This is the 'organisational culture'. 'The first person to arrive brings in the milk', 'We all take turns outside on cold days' or 'We don't do training on our days off', are all examples of organisational culture. Because culture rules are unwritten and, more often than not, unspoken, as a leader you may not even be aware of some of them. The best time to find out about them is during your first few months in the post when you are still asking the question, 'How do we do it here?' This is often when you will get the response, 'We have always done it like this', but when you ask why, you may not get an answer with knowledge, background understanding or conviction.

Often, the most difficult or unpleasant jobs you have to deal with as a leader are the ones linked to capability and disciplinary issues. They are particularly difficult in that they involve saying 'No', 'No, not good enough' or 'No, not acceptable'. Again, it is not only what we say and do but how we say and do it that makes the difference to the outcome.

Capability issues arise when a person is not carrying out their role effectively. Just like a doctor who is presented with a patient's symptoms and then diagnoses the illness before prescribing medication, the Leader as Problem Solver sees the poor performance (symptoms), finds out why the person is not carrying out their duties effectively (diagnosis) and then looks to provide a solution. As discussed in Chapter 3, the leader needs to establish whether it is an issue of ability (capability) or capacity (time, resources, and so on). With regard to capability issues, good recruitment, getting the right person with the right skills, knowledge and attributes, should go a long way in preventing such problems. Good induction procedures, where policies, procedures and expectations are shared and discussed, are another important way to ensure from the outset that organisational expectations are clearly understood.

Disciplinary issues occur when someone breaks, or consistently breaks, an organisational rule or expectation, and these situations are equally unpleasant to deal with. A common issue might be persistent lateness. These issues are usually dealt with in much the same way as capability issues: a reiteration of what is expected, a timeframe for reviewing the situation and an explanation of the consequences if improvement is not made. It is important that leaders act with integrity throughout such processes and are also fair and consistent in applying and following the procedures.

An open, honest recruitment and selection process, together with good induction procedures, should make clear the expectations of the role and the organisation. In this way, if expectations are clear from the outset and reviewed regularly, there should be fewer instances of capability, disciplinary and organisational culture issues and concerns.

Reflection: activity

Helping staff to understand the expectations of their role

Imagine you are new to your setting. Walk around the building and think about your current induction process. As a new team member, how would you find out:

- what you are expected to do in each area of the building?

- about policies and procedures that are related to everyday practice (such as giving children medicine)?

- about policies and procedures that are related to the organisation of the setting (such as what to do when you are ill)?

- about the organisational culture?

- what you are doing well?

- where you need to develop and your plans for improvement?

- what support is available (both inside and outside the setting)?

Think about the induction process at your current place of work. Does it address the above questions, and, if not, what do you need to change or develop?

The worst thing a leader could do is to ignore an identified issue or situation completely. Doing this would send out negative messages to the member of staff involved, who is probably aware of their own areas for development (we are usually our own worst critics), and to the other team members if they are aware of the situation. To accept poor performance and do nothing to improve it could cause serious emotional or physical harm to children and families, and could be damaging to the reputation of the organisation. There may be lots of reasons why you would rather not deal with the situation, but leaders need to have the courage to stand up for what is right (see Chapter 5) and need to challenge and support their teams to deliver high quality (see Chapters 3 and 8).

> The ultimate measure of a man is not where he stands in moments of comfort, but where he stands at times of challenge and controversy.
>
> (Martin Luther King, Jr)

A cautionary note

If you are dealing with performance, capability or disciplinary issues with an individual, it is important that the employee be able to trust the leader to retain confidentiality. Though other team members may need to be aware of the situation, it is not appropriate that this should be discussed publicly; it should be on a 'need to know' basis only.

Building happy and effective teams

Individuals perform best when they have good levels of personal well-being, but what happens when these individuals interact within an organisation and how can we create the conditions to support teams to work together effectively?

Understanding teams

There is a wealth of published work on team dynamics, team building and team relationships. The theory of team development below is one that can put the issues described in this chapter into a theoretical context.

Tuckman's 'Greasy Pole' theory is a very well known way of thinking about team development (and regression). In his 1965 article 'Developmental Sequence in Small Groups', Tuckman explains precisely why teams get into difficulties in the first place, but more importantly states that teams should expect to have periods of disagreement and misunderstandings. Tuckman offers four stages of group development: forming, storming, norming and performing.

> *Groups initially concern themselves with orientation accomplished primarily through testing. Such testing serves to identify the boundaries of both interpersonal and task behaviours. Coincident with testing in the interpersonal realm is the establishment of dependency relationships with leaders, other group members, or pre-existing standards. It may be said that orientation, testing and dependence constitute the group process of* forming.
>
> (Tuckman 2001, p. 8)

At the 'forming' stage, everyone is polite and trying to get to know each other. The team are establishing their own roles and relationships, both within the team and with the leader.

> *The second point in the sequence is characterised by conflict and polarisation around interpersonal issues, with concomitant emotional responding in the task sphere. These behaviours serve as resistance to group influence and task requirements and may be labelled as* storming.

The 'storming' stage happens as an emotional response to team roles, relationships and boundaries. Tuckman's theory expects that teams will experience conflict. This can be heart-warming to a leader: not that there is conflict, but that it is an expected part of being in a team, not simply down to something you, or anyone else, has done or not done.

> *Resistance is overcome in the third stage in which in-group feeling and cohesiveness develop, new standards evolve, and*

new roles are adopted. In the task realm, intimate, personal opinions are expressed. Thus, we have the stage of norming.

The 'norming' stage happens as the team begins to gel. Individuals feel comfortable to say what they think and feel.

Finally, the group attains the fourth and final stage in which interpersonal structure becomes the tool of task activities. Roles become flexible and functional, and group energy is channelled into the task. Structural issues have been resolved, and structure can now become supportive of task performance. This stage can be labelled as performing.

In the 'performing' stage, everyone knows their role. Expectations are met, individuals support each other and offer praise and encouragement. It could be said that at this stage, the team are firing on all cylinders.

Once leaders understand and accept Tuckman's theory on team development it can be easier to manage the process. However, team development does not always start at forming and work its way through to performing. There are factors that influence the team along the way, such as new team members joining, concerns over funding and budgets, tight timescales, and deadlines to be met. This causes the team to move up and down through the stages, a bit like being on a 'greasy pole'. The challenge for the Leader as a Problem Solver is to recognise when to act as the team move up and down the pole, between the four stages.

Tuckman and Jensen (1977) proposed an update of the model, with a fifth stage for which a rhyming word could not be found at the time. The word 'adjourning' was added, and concerns the ending of roles, for example, when the task reaches its conclusion and there is less need for 'management' or when a key person leaves the team. Eventually a rhyming word was found and this stage is now generally known as 'mourning'.

Being aware of organisational culture

Conflict sometimes occurs within a team because organisational culture expectations have not been met. Some aspects of organisational culture will be helpful to the team; norms such as, 'We all help to clear up at the end of the session', others may not, for example, 'Nobody challenges X's decisions' or 'The toddler room staff do not share with the baby room staff'. These negative organisational culture norms can be the cause of low-level conflict and tension within the workplace. They are difficult to identify and difficult to remove. The Leader as a Problem Solver needs to steer a very careful course and act with integrity at all times if they are going to improve negative aspects of organisational culture. Ignoring the situation is not a solution and though role modelling appropriate behaviour will help, it probably will not be enough.

Conflict, debate and discussion within the team

Having established that conflict is not helpful, it would then appear paradoxical to claim that effective teams need to be able to disagree. However, disagreement does not have to mean the same as conflict. In conflict there are sides, points to be scored and battles to be won. This, on the other hand, is about the ability of teams, and members within teams, to debate and potentially disagree. 'Healthy' debates need to be conducted in an emotionally intelligent and supportive manner. Everyone should be encouraged to have their say and be listened to. Issues should be looked at from all viewpoints and finally everyone should come to an agreed way forward.

As a leader you sometimes need to initiate discussions that people are unwilling to start because they do not want to potentially upset the harmony of the team or upset individual team members. Acknowledging and starting to address these issues, thoughts and feelings is sometimes referred to as tackling the 'elephant in the corner' – a thing that everyone knows is there but is unwilling to publicly acknowledge or talk about. The leader needs to be seen to confront issues and support teams to challenge practices in an appropriate manner. Differences of opinion should not make a person feel undermined or a less valuable member of the team. It is acceptable to have strong opinions, but not to intimidate others. Leaders need to support others to understand that it is the ideas that are being debated, not a person's worth. A crucial element of this approach is that once a team decision has been made then everyone has to support the decision and work with it (see also Chapter 4 for more on support and challenge).

There are many advantages to encouraging team dialogue and debate:

managers. When Anne explained this to the rest of the team, comments such as, 'how typical', 'always lets us down', 'never turns up', were made. The team quickly rearranged to cover the missing team member's duties. The delegate feedback was very positive and afterwards Anne took the team for a meal to celebrate.

Scenario B
Anne loved her job as a manager within a large organisation. The role varied daily and offered lots of opportunity for challenge and diversity. When the opportunity to organise a large conference was offered, Anne jumped at the chance. The team were enthusiastic, everyone got involved and the plans came together for a conference that would be fulfilling for the team and the delegates alike. On the day of the conference, everyone pulled together, the delegate feedback was very positive and afterwards Anne took the team for a meal to celebrate.

Both scenarios are normal in working life.

Questions:

- How do you think Anne felt?

- How do you think the team felt?

- What was the impact on the team's motivation?

- How do you think the individual team member would feel upon returning to work?

- How would the scenario affect team dynamics?

- How could you manage this type of situation?

Reflection: case study

Knotty problems

Sally is a family outreach worker, covering several settings within a locality. Sally and her line manager, Yasmin, have worked together for several years and have a good working relationship. Yasmin is aware that Sally has recently separated from her partner, is having trouble coping with a teenage son (as well as a young toddler) and that money is often tight for the family.

One morning Yasmin informs Sally that there has been an incident at The CC Club (one of the settings in Sally's area). Yasmin explains that Sally need no longer attend the parents group at the club. That particular session on her timetable would be filled with other duties. Yasmin explains that the information is confidential and reiterates that Sally should not be worried. Sally takes Yasmin at her word and carries on with her role supporting the families across the area.

Sally tries to ensure she supports Yasmin whenever possible as she is aware that Yasmin is having health issues and awaiting a crucial operation. Six months later, Yasmin has to take time off work and Sally is delighted when she is successful in her application to cover Yasmin's absence.

Whilst Yasmin is absent, Sally is asked to look for a receipt that appears to have gone astray. Sally is sorting through some papers looking for the receipt when she notices a letter from The CC Club. Sally is about to file the letter when she notices her own name in bold type. Sally reads the letter and is distraught when she realises that it is a complaint from the club: the incident referred to by Yasmin six months previously was in fact a complaint against Sally.

Questions:

- How do you think Sally feels?

- Why do you think Yasmin did not mention the complaint?

- How would you have managed the above situation?

- If you were Yasmin and Sally's line manager, how would you take this forward?

Reflection: activity

Diary of interactions

Over a one-week period, compile your daily interactions with your staff team using copies of the grid below to monitor who you talk to and why. Use a new grid for each day so that you are not influenced by your notes from previous days. There should be just a quick note for each interaction.

Who:	Which team member?
	If you instigated the conversation put a circle – O – next to the name. If the team member instigated it put a ✓
Where:	In the building, outside, on the phone after work, etc.
Why:	Why did the interaction take place? – leadership, management, social, emotional, etc.
When:	Time of day

How long:

Was the interaction:	brief? (less than five minutes)
	standard? (between five and fifteen minutes)
	lengthy? (over twenty minutes)
	in-depth? (over forty-five minutes)
Rating of comfort level:	How did you feel about the interaction? (1 = anxious to 6 = very comfortable)

Diary of interactions

Day:

Who	Where	Why	When	How long	Rating

After one week compare the different days and assess the following points:

- Who do you interact with on a daily/weekly basis?

- Why do most of your interactions take place?

- Are your interactions always in response to issues/concerns; are you simply 'fire-fighting'?

- Who instigates most of the interactions?

- Where do most of the interactions take place?

- Are they at specific times of the day?

- Do they last different lengths of time depending on who you are with?

- How comfortable do you feel talking to each person?

Communicating with your team

The data from the above activity should give you some idea of the way you interact with each of your team members. If you work in a large organisation it may be that you do not have line management responsibility for all of the employees, or you may work in a building where your team is one of several. In cases such as these, you need to make the effort to know the names of people in other teams as well as all the ancillary staff. Staff who do not work directly with children should be given the opportunity to feel part of the team. Team members should be encouraged to attend staff meetings and staff functions, and have the opportunity to be involved in making decisions about their work. As leader you need to ensure that staff have access to supervision, appraisal and continuous professional development opportunities. Finally, they need to know what your organisational improvement priorities are and how they could or do contribute (see Chapter 8).

Reflection: activity

Question	Team member	Reflections?
Who do you spend most time interacting with?		
Who do you spend least time interacting with?		
Are there any team members you only have positive interactions with?		
Are there members of your team that you only have negative interactions with?		
Is there someone you have not spoken to at all? And if so, why?		

Question	Team member	Reflections?
Are there people you avoid?		
During the conversations, were any decisions made? If so, who made them?		
Have you spent the week just giving instructions to a particular member of the team?		
Was anyone else involved in the interactions?		
Do you have team members who you only interact with if they are not on their own?		

- Did you expect the answers you have?
- Are there any surprises?
- How do you feel looking back at the interactions?
- Are there areas you need to address?

What do the above answers tell you about how you communicate with your team?

Looking after the leader

Leaders and managers have the power to influence other people's needs and feelings. You may well have worked with people who have abused this power.

Power is an emotive word to which we can respond in a number of ways:

- we may be desperate for it
  - (I cannot make any decisions)

- we may be self-conscious about it
  - (I do not have power: we are all equals)

- we may grasp it with both hands
  - (I am the manager: what I say goes).

Alternatively, we may be elsewhere on the continuum.

In an organisational context, power is often associated with words such as control, authority, rule and command. This may or may not be how you see your role.

Does the team see you as the boss, the manager or as a superior? If they (or you) think of the leadership role in that way it may make it difficult for them to see (or for you to show) your vulnerabilities, needs and feelings. Previous sections have looked at caring for teams and understanding their needs and motivations. Even though not top of the list, the team still need to see you as a person with needs and feelings. If you do not allow this, there is a danger of your relationship with them becoming a power relationship. This could influence the happiness and equilibrium of the team.

It is also worth thinking about how the image of leadership as a power relationship could shape other areas of work. For example, if members of your team see leadership in this way (because of your words or actions, or because of prior experience), it may take some perseverance to get them to act on their own initiative and suggest changes, which will then have an influence on CQI, the development of relationships with children and families, and so on. It is also likely to be a barrier to an effective working relationship.

Leaders often say, 'I would not ask anyone in my team to do something I am not prepared to do myself'. But often as leaders we do things that we would not expect of others: working long hours, doing our own jobs while covering for absent colleagues, and forgoing breaks, are common examples. As leaders we often take on much more than we would expect of others and by default we deny our own needs and feelings. Leaders need to ensure that they have the physical and emotional reserves to effectively support others.

Leaders being asked to make 'urgent' decisions

This section links to the section on questioning in Chapter 2, only this time it is about when you are on the receiving end of being questioned. This can be quite daunting, particularly to someone who is new to a leadership position.

There are many occasions when people rush up to leaders and demand an answer to something they need to know immediately. Whilst there are circumstances that require immediate action, many do not, and you could find yourself being pushed into making a snap decision that later proves to be wrong. When someone stops you in the car park/lift/toilet demanding an immediate response – for example, 'Can I attend training in six months time?', 'What are you going to do as someone missed their turn on the washing up rota?', 'Who are you going to send to the conference, can I go?' – calmly say that you are pleased they have brought this to your attention, that you will get back to them in a day or two when you have had time to think about it, or say, 'Good suggestion. Bring it to the team meeting where we can discuss it together.'

Being at the receiving end of such questioning can be hugely distracting and can also reinforce the notion that it is the leader's responsibility to solve all problems. The technique mentioned above works on many levels and people soon get the message.

- It stops people running up to you in inappropriate places asking you to deal with things.
- It stops individuals trying to gain an unfair advantage.
- It stops you making snap decisions and then having to change your mind later when you have more information.
- It buys you time to think: who else and what else do you need to consider?

Reflection: activity

Where can leaders find social and supportive relationships?

Leaders need to recognise their own needs, weaknesses and vulnerabilities if they are going to help themselves, the organisation and ultimately the main stakeholders in the organisation (practitioners, children and families). By doing this they are in a better position to look for, ask for or accept support. So the Leader as a Problem Solver needs to be able to self-reflect and understand where and when support is required and hopefully where it can be found. The saying 'a problem shared is a problem halved' is relevant in this case. As a leader you should be able to ask for help from your team and others, delegate responsibility and able to accept offers of help.

As leader, you need to be aware of where you can go to for:

- a critical friend/mentor
- a sounding board for ideas
- fast decision making
- talking out problems (whether or not you want a solution)
- confidential discussions
- emotional support.

Which of these roles you take on for other people?

No leader is perfect. The best ones don't try to be – they concentrate on honing their strengths and find others who can make up for their limitations.

(Ancona and others 2007, p. 2)

Chapter summary

The Leader as a Problem Solver knows that prevention is better than cure, looks for potential issues, and tries to eliminate the risk of them occurring. When issues arise, the leader needs to have strategies to deal with them, but also needs to have attributes such as courage to stand up for what is right and to ensure that the values and ethos of the organisation are embodied in day-to-day practice.

Leaders need to ensure good two-way communication with stakeholders in order to establish expectations. How leaders deal with compliments, complaints and consultation is important.

Leaders should support staff to meet the expectations of their roles through procedures such as induction, supervision, appraisal and other methods of feedback.

Awareness of theory of team development and dynamics can support leaders deal with conflict within teams and to build and strengthen them. Leaders need to support and challenge teams to build their problem solving capacity and to work effectively together, caring for each other and building a strong network of relationships.

Awareness of quality improvement approaches can help leaders plan and implement improvement.

Leaders know that they cannot do everything and that they will not always be right. They should be able to acknowledge this and ask for support when necessary.

8 The Leader as a Developer

Quality is never an accident.
It is always the result of intelligent effort.

(John Ruskin)

The Leader as a Developer

Effective leaders promote a culture of continuous quality improvement (CQI). They encourage practitioners and other stakeholders to be reflective and to suggest and implement improvements. They enable the sharing of good practice and networking with other organisations.

This chapter looks at the leader's role in raising, developing and maintaining quality in early years and playwork settings. It explores the meaning of Continuous Quality Improvement (CQI), why organisational development is important, how we might go about embedding CQI in our organisations and the dispositions or qualities of leadership that are helpful in the CQI process. The chapter also looks at how we might go about measuring the impact of our activities to identify whether or not we have improved quality and made any difference to the stakeholders we serve.

Leadership is an essential part of quality improvement

The *Children's Plan* (DCSF 2007) states:

> *Leaders in the early years sector need to set a clear vision for quality and improvement in settings and lead a positive learning culture in which all staff continually reflect on and improve their practice. They also need to be committed to learning from the best. Leaders in a world class early years sector will be instrumental in embedding continuous quality improvement in settings – thus focusing on the needs of every individual child – but also in helping to shape and raise parents' expectations of the quality they can expect from early learning.*

(Para 34)

Leadership is an essential part of quality improvement and quality improvement is a key function of leaders. In essence, quality improvement is about change; moving from one state of being to another. If that change is to be purposeful and move ever closer towards improved outcomes for all children, and narrowing the gap between the most vulnerable children and the rest, then strong leadership is required. In *Narrowing the Gap in Outcomes: Leadership* (2009, pp. iv–v), Martin and others highlight six key ingredients required of leaders to narrow the gap:

- *Prioritising the most vulnerable and developing a local vision*

- *Championing the voice of vulnerable groups and encouraging their participation*

- *Using good quality data to identify needs and provide services for vulnerable groups*

- *Fostering partnership working around vulnerable groups*

- *Developing and motivating the workforce to improve outcomes for vulnerable groups*

- *Having an unrelenting drive and passion to improve outcomes for vulnerable groups.*

The basis of these six key ingredients could also be applied to leadership in general when undertaking any kind of quality improvement activity. Chapter 5 discussed the leader's responsibility for developing a shared vision within the organisation. The leader needs to be able to tell the organisation's story – where it has come from, where it wants to go and how it is going to get there. The clearer that picture or vision of the future state, the more likely it is that others will be able to share and commit to the vision and work together to achieve it. 'Begin with the end in mind' (Covey 1992 p. 98): having a vision of how things will be is a key element of Outcomes Based Accountability (OBA) that will be examined closely later in this chapter.

Martin and others go on to say:

> Effective leaders ensure that staff have an understanding of the vision for narrowing the gap, and that improving outcomes is a priority for them. They make it clear to the workforce how their roles contribute to improving outcomes. They work to develop the emotional connection of staff with vulnerable young people and encourage and facilitate the sharing of good practice.
>
> (2009, p. 15)

Defining quality and quality improvement activity

Quality

When we think about quality, we have different opinions about the relative importance of different aspects or ingredients of the product or service we are considering. Garvin (1984, p. 26) gives five categories for the ways that people think about quality, which can be applied to early years settings.

1. *Transcendent:* This is related to perceived 'premium products', and might be a very exclusive and expensive childcare setting.
2. *Product-based:* This refers to the 'ingredients' that make up the product or service. In terms of childcare, this could be the quality of the building, the level of staff qualifications, the number of staff, the meals provided, the hours of opening, and so on.
3. *User-based:* This is understood as what the customer wants. Parents may want to know that their child will be loved and that

they have access to a childcare provision they can walk to, with flexible hours – all for a manageable price. This definition relies on knowing who your customer groups are (including internal customers, the staff).

4. *Manufacturing-based:* This looks at the quality of the manufactured product, so in terms of childcare we might look at the outcomes for children or the setting's Ofsted judgement.

5. *Value-based:* This last definition acknowledges that cost needs to be taken into consideration as well as customer requirements. Its goal is to provide the best product or service possible, given the amount customers can afford to pay, i.e., value for money.

The third and fifth definitions are possibly the most useful in the early years and playwork sector. However, that does not negate the fact that some people will always think of quality products as the most exclusive (rather than the most inclusive) and some people will use rating systems such as Ofsted judgements and league tables as their only benchmarks for quality.

Documents such as *Your Child's Early Learning and Care: Birth to Five – Ideas and Support for You* (DCSF 2009b) are useful in supporting parents to understand how they might go about choosing quality provision that meets their needs.

Quality control

This is where products or services are checked against specified criteria and is most often found in a manufacturing environment. It is usually seen as an internal organisational method for managing quality, for example, the processes used to 'spot check' procedures. In early years and playwork, quality control could also be used to describe regulation and inspection processes as well as organisational or local authority moderation processes used to check practitioners' judgements about children's progress.

Quality assurance

Quality assurance (QA) aims to assure customers that the quality of the product or service is of a good or high standard and has been verified by an external body. Early years and playwork have local authority and sector specific schemes, for example, the National Childminding Association's (NCMA) Quality First for childminders. Some organisations may also choose to undertake schemes such as Investors in People (www.investorsinpeople.co.uk) that are not specific to early years or playwork.

Leaders and managers like to use quality assurance as a way of systematically looking at all aspects of their provision. It can be particularly useful for those who are new to a leadership role or new to quality improvement activity, as schemes usually include an element of mentor support. For teams who have been together for a while, undertaking a QA journey can be a way of re-energising and refocusing. For others, the rigidity of QA schemes is constraining and following a scheme is seen as diverting attention from other more important quality improvement issues. Settings who are undertaking a quality assurance scheme are encouraged to include this information in their Ofsted Self Evaluation Form. Of settings who have achieved a QA award, Ofsted say there is 'a clearer focus on excellent commitment and systems to improve quality' (Ofsted 2008, p. 59).

Continuous Quality Improvement

The concept of quality improvement or continuous quality improvement (CQI) acknowledges that organisations have different starting points but that it is the process or journey that is important and the culture of continuously striving to improve. This is also recognised in the Ofsted framework where settings are now also judged on leadership and management and their capacity to improve. 'Continuous' refers to the idea that improvement should be ongoing and not a discrete activity.

CQI also recognises that there are many ways to improve quality and that these may or may not include quality control and quality assurance. Other ways of developing quality could include continuous professional development opportunities, accredited training, and support and challenge from the local authority or a sector-specific development worker. Settings may use a specific approach to improving quality. For example, the Early Years Quality Improvement Support Programme (EYQISP) materials (DCSF 2008a) offer a 'setting improvement cycle'. Outcomes Based Accountability (OBA) is another approach to improving quality (see p. 116) that focuses on the quality of end results or 'outcomes' rather than just focusing on the processes used to achieve the outcomes. This approach to improving quality is gaining popularity in children's services, particularly when working in multi-agency teams.

Why undertake quality improvement?

The reasons given by many organisations for quality improvement activity are as follows:

- producing better products or services
- market place positioning – improving the reputation and sustainability of the organisation
- cost efficiency – getting a better yield for money spent and reducing the costs associated with poor quality.

In children's services, whether you work in a for-profit or a not-for-profit organisation, the above reasons could apply to your involvement in quality improvement activities. Without a sufficient number of service users or customers, organisations are not viable. The last bullet point runs hand-in-hand with the first two and entails using resources efficiently – this could be funding, equipment and/or personnel. The costs associated with poor quality could be cut by reducing the number of complaints and concerns, hence reducing the amount of time (and money) spent putting things right.

The organisation could also be made more cost efficient by reducing the amount of wastage – this might be of food at meal and snack times, of equipment that has not been properly looked after, or of time, for example, in replicating work, using overly complicated processes or on training that has little or no impact on provision.

It is important that quality improvement initiatives are congruent with values. For example, it might save time to change children's nappies conveyor belt style, but that might not sit comfortably with, say, the organisation's goal of treating each child as unique or fostering positive relationships. In this case, key people spending more time with each child and using nappy changing as valuable communication time would be a more appropriate indicator of quality.

CQI in early years and playwork settings

With the introduction of the Early Years Foundation Stage (DfES 2007) and the Ofsted Inspection Framework (Ofsted 2008), there is an expectation that all early years and playwork settings will engage in CQI activities. Settings are expected to self-evaluate using a range of tools, identify areas for improvement and evaluate the impact that existing improvement activities have made.

There is a further expectation that settings should consult with their stakeholders, specifically, children, parents and staff, and should involve them in the completion of the Ofsted Self Evaluation Form. Ofsted inspection reports give judgements on the quality of leadership and management and the setting's capacity to improve as well as its ability to deliver good outcomes for children and families.

Will self-evaluation by settings have an impact on the quality of provision and on outcomes for children and families? In their research on integrating self-assessment into statutory inspection procedures, Munton and Mooney state that:

> ... self-assessment, even when part of statutory inspection procedures, is unlikely to have a uniformly positive impact on the quality of all provision, at least in the short term. Consistent with research from the US and Australia, it would appear that improvements in quality are closely linked to the ability of providers to plan and implement changes in working practices.
>
> Where providers do not have key organisational characteristics such as participatory management styles, a committed workforce satisfied with their working conditions, opportunities for in-service training and a positive attitude towards innovation, encouraging self-assessment is unlikely to have a significant impact on quality.
>
> (2001, p. 37)

Munton and Mooney have identified that simply expecting settings to complete a self-evaluation will not necessarily bring about improvement to their quality. The conditions required to bring about quality improvement are complex, while the skills required include being able to accurately identify the strengths and weaknesses of the organisation (self-assessment) and the ability to plan and implement changes.

- How is feedback used? Is giving and receiving of feedback used as a way to *mentor* and support individuals and teams?

- How do you create opportunities for your teams to have autonomy to develop and *champion* their own projects?

- How do you use challenge and change to *motivate* people, rather than cause frustration?

- How do you support people to analyse and interpret information, reach agreements and *problem solve* to find their own answers?

- How do you delegate responsibility to *develop* others' skills, knowledge and understanding?

- How does the above support you and your team to engage in CQI?

How do you lead for quality; developing, supporting and encouraging others to be a part of CQI? How do you develop the leadership skills of others? The Leader as a Developer knows that one way to develop CQI is to develop the leaders of the future and support them to lead for quality too.

Learning by sharing: learning from others and being an advocate of your own practice

In order to evaluate quality you need to have an idea of what good quality is and be able to compare that with your own practice. The Leader as a Developer understands this and looks for ways to enable it to happen. Visits to other settings and networking opportunities are good ways to gain new ideas and compare aspects of practice.

Having people visit your organisation helps you to think about what you are doing and why you are doing it. Being questioned about your practice means you have to explain and justify it and the focus of the questions may give you another angle from which to assess the quality of your practice. It is as important for practitioners to visit other provision and talk about their own practice to visitors (including prospective parents) as it is for leaders to visit and show people around. Much confidence can be gained by practitioners through this process and the value gained from fresh ideas to invigorate practice is immense.

Enabling the whole team to learn from experience

Chapter 2 discussed the importance of the leader creating an environment where individuals feel able to take risks and try out new ideas. The Leader as a Developer needs to encourage all staff to suggest and implement changes to enhance the quality of provision. To achieve this, the leader needs to create a culture within which the boundaries and principles that guide and shape work are understood. In this way the leader does not restrict or inhibit ideas and innovation, but creates a safety net or a safe place within which to work and develop practice.

Products, processes and outcomes

When looking for quality in the range of organisational processes and outcomes, the Leader as a Developer is responsible for crystallising the vision (Senge and others 2005, p. 133) and creating the conditions that encourage and enable improvement to happen. These improvements can be thought of as products, processes and outcomes. Examples of products (things that have been produced by the organisation) include the layout of the environment, the menu or the newsletter. Processes could include how children are welcomed at the beginning of a session or how budgets are set and managed. The improved outcomes will be different for each stakeholder group and for the individuals within those groups. They might include, for example, a better qualified workforce, flexible provision or a better working partnership for parents, and more participation, independence and choice for children.

Outcomes are achieved through products and processes. If we take the example of the better qualified workforce, some of the processes linked to it might be: supervision and appraisal, workplace mentoring, supply cover procedures, allocation of training budgets, pre- and post-training interviews and planning.

Any organisation will have hundreds of procedures and processes, some written and some unwritten. The Leader as a Developer needs to reflect on the quality, consistency and effectiveness of these processes, but, more importantly, needs to enable the team to reflect on them and correct, adjust or improve them as necessary. This is essential as the leader cannot be everywhere at once. Processes, procedures and services in general cannot be put aside to be inspected later when the leader has time to do it. They are produced at the point of delivery and therefore need to be 'inspected' by the person providing the process or service (changing a nappy, greeting a family, and so on).

Part of a process versus being processed

In a time when Ofsted inspections focus on the experience of the child – 'What is it like for a child here?' – it is worth reflecting on Black and Wiliam's concept of the classroom as a 'black box'; a type of machine with inputs and outputs. They warn us about the negative effects caused by some of our processes (inputs), for example, assessments, and the pressure put on pupils and practitioners to achieve better outcomes (outputs). They ask us to consider the experience of pupils and practitioners 'inside the black box':

In terms of systems engineering, present policy seems to treat the classroom as a black box.

Certain inputs *from the outside are fed in or make demands – pupils, teachers, other resources, management rules and requirements, parental anxieties, tests with pressures to score highly, and so on.*

Some outputs *follow, hopefully pupils who are more knowledgeable and competent, better test results, teachers who are more or less satisfied, and more or less exhausted.*

(Black and Wiliam 2001, p. 1)

Black and Wiliam believe that this type of assessment is unhelpful and that we should be moving towards more formative assessment frameworks. The questions raised about systems 'inside the black box' could also be applied to approaches to quality improvement in the early years and playwork sector. Black and Wiliam go on to say:

But what is happening inside? How can anyone be sure that a particular set of new inputs will produce better outputs if we don't at least study what happens inside?

(Black and Wiliam 2001, p. 1)

It can feel as if more inputs are being produced and more outputs expected. It is important to consider 'what happens inside'.

Measuring outcomes – have you made a difference?

Increased public funding for children's services in the twenty-first century is coupled with increased expectations of improved outcomes and accountability for the money spent. Organisations spend huge amounts of time and money measuring the quality of the services they offer without always understanding the relationship between the processes and the outcomes. For example, a child attending nursery does not necessarily correlate to improved learning for that child. Or, just because a setting has parents' evenings does not mean that all parents are involved in their children's learning. If the desired outcome is that children learn more or that parents are more involved, there should be a variety of different indicators or measures to let us know that we are travelling in the right direction.

Outcomes Based Accountability (also known as Results Accountability) is a system of producing measurable improvements that was devised by Mark Friedman in 2005. When charting the progress of quality improvement activities, Friedman asks the question, 'Is anyone better off?' This idea sits well with the expectation of the Ofsted Self Evaluation Form that we evaluate the impact of quality improvement activities. In other words, when we describe quality improvements we need to think about the difference it has made.

The OBA approach is gaining popularity in children's services in England and has been adopted by organisations such as DCSF, the Centre for Excellence and Outcomes (C4EO) and NCB. For a more detailed explanation of OBA see Friedman, 2005 or visit www.resultsaccountability.com or www.c4eo.org.uk/obatoolkit.

Getting from talk to action

In OBA planning, groups should be able to transition from talk to action within an hour. A whole range of stakeholders should be represented. The OBA approach recommends the wearing of 'two hats' (that is, looking at the issue from your own perspective and also from that of a stakeholder not represented in the group) in order to help you think differently if you fail initially to attract representation from all key stakeholder groups. The approach offers a simple stepped approach to planning that can be done in almost any order but must start with the end in mind, that is, 'What do we want to achieve?' and should end with, 'What are we going to do?'. See Performance accountability figure below.

Performance Accountability: Getting from talk to action

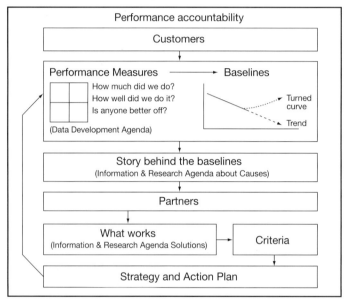

Reproduced with permission from Friedman, Mark (2005) *Trying Hard is not Good Enough: How to produce measurable improvements for customers and communities.* Victoria, BC: Trafford.

Friedman recommends that in order to embed the approach within organisations, leaders and managers should ask the seven performance accountability questions routinely in supervisions. These are:

1. Who are our customers?
2. How can we measure if our customers are better off?
3. How can we measure if we are delivering our services well?
4. How are we doing on the most important of these measures?
5. Who are the partners that have a role to play in doing better?
6. What works to do better, including no-cost and low cost ideas?
7. What do we propose to do?

The DCSF (2008b, para 21) draws attention to the fact that cultural change is necessary if outcomes are to be given the importance necessary to make a difference. About leadership and OBA they say:

Accountability for outcomes requires strong, sustainable leadership. An initial surge of interest will not be enough to make a difference. Leadership must be sustained and capable of surviving changes in senior management.

Using data

'Data' is another word for 'information' and does not necessarily refer to pages of numbers. As a leader you will need to interpret a wide range of data and help others understand it and the implications of it for your provision. This information can be collected by data experts or by you in the setting. It can be extremely accurate or simply an impression. It can be numerical, in graph form, in pictures or in words. Collecting and analysing data is an important aspect of leading and managing early years and playwork settings. For example, you are expected to seek the views of children, parents and staff in order to complete the Ofsted Self Evaluation Form. When evaluating how well your organisation helps to keep children safe, one of the things you might do is to analyse the data on accidents in the setting.

As with other quality improvement approaches, OBA relies on the collection and interpretation of data. When leading quality improvement you may find that you have either too little or too much data. If you have too little, you may be able to rely on what your experience tells you to get started, then concentrate on creating data to help you understand whether on not you are making a difference (performance measures). Having too much data can also cause anxiety. Here it is important to reflect on what information is required to help you understand what you did, how you did it and if anyone was better off as a result – the last being the most important. Discussing school change, Stoll and Fink (1996, p. 65) caution about 'the importance of collecting only a manageable amount of information and the need for interpretation training'.

DCSF (2009a, p. 15) refers to data collection and interpretation on children's progress, but it could apply equally to the progress of other change initiatives.

When information is organised in a systematic way, it helps leaders and managers ask pertinent questions and gives starting points for discussing and understanding progress, and evaluating quality and impact. Leaders and managers should be clear about:

- *what data is collected*

- *how data is collected*

- *what it is used for.*

Planning for quality improvement

Large-scale change projects take up a lot of energy, time and resources. Sometimes the impact is small compared to the amount of effort, and often the change is not sustainable, simply because of the amount of effort required to keep it going. Compare this to the small changes you have been involved in. They are sometimes so small that on their own they do not have much impact.

There are situations, however, where lots of small changes together make for a big and lasting impact. Gladwell (2000) calls the point at which the small things cause a big difference the 'Tipping Point'. In prioritising change, it may be more manageable and sustainable in the long term to opt for the small incremental changes. The skill of the Leader as a Developer is to be aware of the point at which the many small actions start to have a big impact on practice and outcomes.

Reflection: activity

Developing improvement priorities

Think about the issues where you want to make a big impact (your improvement priorities). For example, this might be to improve partnership in working with parents or to improve communication, language and literacy outcomes for boys. It is likely that these issues will be addressed with a range of actions, some large and some small. As a leader you will be aware of the overall quality improvement strategy and the ways in which small changes contribute to this. But do all the staff, including, for example, the support staff recognise the part they are playing in meeting these priorities? These questions may help to start you thinking:

- What are your organisation's improvement priorities?

- How have you involved the whole team in identifying, prioritising and action planning for these improvements?

- Does everyone in your organisation know what their role is (including any staff not working directly with children)?

- Can each person in your organisation describe what they do that contributes towards these improvement priorities?

- Does each person in your organisation have an understanding of the progress that has been made towards achieving the improvements?

- For each of the questions above, what could you do as a leader to improve the situation?

- How are parents and children supported to be involved in the whole quality improvement process?

Action planning for improvement

There is a saying that if you 'fail to plan, you plan to fail'. We all have different ways of organising ourselves; some people write lists and make written plans, others have a mental 'to do' list. When working with others it is important that we have a shared understanding of what is required. Having a written document means that we have more clarity about the planned way ahead and are able to ask more focused questions. It also means having a better understanding about who will be held accountable for specific aspects of the plan and how they will be held accountable.

A good action plan is a working document that tells the story of where you have come from, where you want to be and how you are planning to get there. It helps to clarify what everyone's role is in making the required changes and acts as a reminder to all concerned. As you progress through your course of action and start to cross-off or highlight the completed actions, it tells the story of how far you have travelled on your journey towards the desired outcome.

When writing an action plan it is important to have the end in mind (Covey 1992, p. 97, Friedman 2005, p. 17) and knowing what you want to achieve. In order to achieve a single outcome you will probably have to undertake a range of activities. For each of these activities, identify who will be responsible, the resources required, realistic timescales and how you will monitor progress. It is a good idea to post the plan where it can be seen by everyone. Think about how you will let other stakeholders such as parents know about your plans and the progress you are making. See pp. 146–148 for a quality improvement action plan with questions and a blank version of the same. Start with the first and last columns then complete the sections in between.

Quality improvement action plan

Context: (What and why?)	Activity: (actions)	Responsibilities: (who will lead?)	Resources: (time, money, people, etc.)	Timescales:	Monitoring:	Outcomes?
What is the current situation?	What are we going to do?	Who is going to lead on the activity?	What will we need to do the job?	What are the timescales?	What are the progress indicators along the way?	Where do we want to be?
What is the issue?	How are we going to get there?	Who will ensure that stakeholders are actively involved?	Are there funding implications?	What are the milestones?	How can we monitor who is doing what and their success?	What will it look like? How will people behave, etc.?
Rationale for change: (Why are we doing this?) Why do we need to make this change?		Who needs to be involved?	Who could help? Where will we find sources of support?	When do we need to be complete or halfway through, etc.?		How will we know we are there? How can we review impact?
Links to key docs: EYFS, ECM, Play Principles, etc.	What and how?	Who?	Who and what?	When?	How well are we doing?	So what?

Questions to ask: Yourself Your team Sample questions:						
There may be others you want to add. What are your stakeholders' views on the issue? Does everyone know why the improvements need to take place?	How have you involved the whole team, partners, children and parents in identifying, prioritising and action planning for these improvements? Does everyone in your organisation know what the priorities are (including any staff not working directly with children)?	Can each person in your organisation describe what they do that contributes towards these improvement priorities?	Do you know where to go for support and guidance: for your team and for yourself?	Does everyone know what they need to do and when?	Does each person in your organisation have an understanding of the progress that has been made towards achieving the improvements?	When will you know if you have achieved what you set out to do? When will you review and evaluate?

Blank version: Quality Improvement Action Plan

Context/priority: (What and why?) What was the project?	What and how? Activity: (actions)	Who? Responsibilities: (who will lead?)	Who and what? Resources: (time, money, people, etc)	When? Timescales:	How? Monitoring:	So what? Outcomes?
Rationale for change: (Why did you choose this project?)	Action 1					
	Action 2					
What are the links to key documents: (EYFS, ECM, EYQISP, QA etc)	Action 3					
	Action 4					

Managing change

Chapter 7 refers to quality improvement cycles. The involvement of the whole team in change processes is also discussed. One of the issues for leaders in times of great change is how to avoid overloading the team and inducing change fatigue ('not another change') or stress ('I cannot cope with another change'). The Leader as a Developer needs to use their judgement to find an appropriate pace of change for the organisation. This pace will not always be constant and may be quicker or slower in different parts of the organisation according to need and the ability to implement change.

How you view change depends on how you see the world (see Chapter 1). At one end of the spectrum are those who believe change can be planned and implemented in exactly the way set out; that you can truly 'manage change'. Then there are those at the other end of the spectrum who believe that change cannot be 'managed', only lived or coped with. They believe that when you plan a course of action you must endeavour to navigate in that direction, dealing with events and unexpected challenges along the way. In between these will be other views.

However you view change, it is helpful to be aware of some of the theory of change management. This may enable you to reflect on your strategies and, in particular, on the attitudes and behaviours of your team with regard to proposed or implemented changes.

The change process

Michael Fullan (2007, p. 66) talks about three broad stages in the change process:

- initiation
- implementation
- institutionalisation.

Initiation is taking the decision to make the changes. This process could be short or lengthy, it could be imposed externally or decided internally. This stage includes information gathering and processes for getting agreement for the proposed changes.

Implementation is putting changes in place. Depending on the size and complexity of the changes and the initial starting points, this stage could last several years (think about the introduction of the EYFS).

Institutionalisation is when the change either becomes embedded in practice or a decision is made to stop the initiative.

The change process is, essentially, 'plan, do, review', and most changes can be categorised in this way. The skill of the leader is in judging how much time and effort needs to be spent on each phase or stage. For example, at the initiation stage, if you spend too much time thinking about and perfecting your action plan you may never get round to actually implementing it. On the other hand, if you spend too little time helping others to understand the need for change and hurry into implementation, you may end up with a very unhappy team who are not committed to the change.

Attitudes to change

Sometimes we are involved in change that we have initiated or welcomed. At other times, change, or the need to change, is imposed externally. Responses to externally imposed change can vary hugely. Individual circumstances can have an effect on people's resilience and ability to adapt to change (see Maslow's Hierarchy of Needs, p. 87). We can all think of people who thrive on change and novelty and of others who find change extremely challenging.

In the 1970s, Elisabeth Kubler-Ross developed the 'change curve'. This curve plots how people in mourning go through the emotions of shock, denial, fear, anger, depression and finally acceptance before they are able to move on. Although originally developed to describe the mourning process, it is now widely acknowledged as relevant to how some people go through the process of change. Some people embrace change and enjoy challenge in the workplace, not displaying these behaviours and emotions at all. Others get stuck in the process and find it difficult to move on. The rate of progress through the stages could be different for different members of a team and, at any one time within an organisation, different people may be at different stages. It also helps to remember that if staff are expressing emotions such as anger, it may be a necessary part of the process.

Being aware of the possibility of these strong reactions to change may make it easier for the leader to acknowledge them, to give staff space and time to express their feelings and help them understand the reasons for and benefits of change. We can compare this process to when a child is separated from a parent; the child goes through a similar range of strong emotions such as fear and anger – the practitioner acknowledges and 'contains' the emotion for the child.

It is important that the leader give staff both the physical and emotional space and time to discuss, challenge, disagree, come to a compromise or change their mind. Sometimes that space for discussion and dialogue needs to be away from the leader. At this point it may be worth thinking about the staff room. If you are the manager of the setting, do you check with them before spending time in their space? If you lead in a different capacity, for example as room leader, how do you give your team space to discuss without you?

Reflection: activity

Emotions in the change process

Think about a recent change in your workplace.

Are you able to identify the different stages that different members of your team were at during their approach to the change?

Can you identify what you as a leader should do to empower each team member to move on to the next stage, and ultimately 'move on'?

Motivation to change

Chapter 1 looked at the 'carrot and stick' approach of the transactional leader. Whilst this approach (reward or fear) may work in the short term, it is unlikely to work in the long term, or to be self-perpetuating, that is, work without constant supervision and application of the rewards and sanctions. Discussing motivation to change, Fullan (2007, p. 42), quoting Deutschman (2005), says that even when faced with stark decisions such as 'change or die' or given compelling moral reasons to change, people are unlikely to do so unless their emotions, and not just their thoughts, are influenced.

It is important to give people the opportunity and the skills to be reflective (influencing thought) and also to give them the opportunity to put this reflection into action (influencing behaviour). Within this process there lies motivation. Where people feel emotionally connected to the change, it is far more likely to take place and be sustainable. Senge (2006, p. 203) recognised this when he talked about 'enrolling' and committing to a vision rather than 'buying in' to someone else's vision. Helping individuals form their personal vision that is congruent with the collective vision is an important aspect of leadership. The challenge of the Leader as a Developer is to encourage those emotional connections.

> *Effective leaders ensure that staff have an understanding of the vision for narrowing the gap, and that improving outcomes is a priority for them. They make it clear to the workforce how their roles contribute to improving outcomes. They work to develop the emotional connection of staff with vulnerable young people and encourage and facilitate the sharing of good practice.*
>
> (Martin and others 2009, p. 15)

Barriers and resistance to change

Often when introducing change, leaders encounter barriers and resistance. There are some who will be convinced that it is change for change's sake, others who feel that there is nothing wrong with what they do currently, and still others who feel that what they have done for years works well enough and does not need changing. Below are a few of the reasons why individuals may feel this way:

- they have a low tolerance for change
- they have had negative past experiences of change
- they feel threatened, for example, by loss of status or influence, loss of pay or loss of comfort zone
- they do not feel that the proposed change fits in with their vision and values
- they feel the change will not be in the best interests of the stakeholders or the organisation, or will cause negative outcomes not yet foreseen.

The Leader as a Developer needs to be aware of these objections and to respond to them appropriately. If a member of staff has a strong aversion to change then it might be helpful to forewarn them and be prepared to give additional support to get them through the change period. If a member of staff thinks that change efforts are a waste of time because things always go back to the way they were (or worse), then you will have to be patient and persevere to earn that person's trust.

People who resist change because it is not in their best interest to make the change are perhaps the most difficult to deal with. They may not make direct challenges to the change process but may try and influence others – getting them to change their point of view and add to the resistance effort. These leaders of resistance are often referred to as 'saboteurs'. Books on change management will recommend that when embarking on change projects, leaders identify and contain the negative activity of the saboteurs in their organisation whilst at the same time identifying those who relish change and are capable of leading and encouraging others to make the desired changes.

Although not comfortable or convenient, challenges and searching questions can sometimes be helpful in order to see the proposed changes from other points of view. It is useful to have diversity in ways of thinking in the workforce. When a strong challenge is made, the Leader as a Developer needs to pay particular heed to the member of staff and listen not only to the objection, but also to why the person feels as they do. Activities that call for multiple perspectives such as de Bono's Six Thinking Hats (see p. 48) and OBA help you see prospective changes from different view points. A SWOT (strengths, weaknesses, opportunities and threats) analysis for a proposed course of action can also help clarify any potential risks.

Reflection: case study

Barriers to change: case study A

Marcie, the deputy manager of a full daycare setting, has been informed by senior line managers that the team will be expected to expand their current work to include a new project. The team are used to taking on board new initiatives and thrive on the challenge.

At the team meeting, Marcie explains the new project and asks for two volunteers to attend a conference to learn more about the project and how it will be monitored and evaluated. Selma and Tomas offer to attend; this is agreed by the rest of the team. Marcie then spends the rest of the meeting facilitating the discussion on how the project can be incorporated into current roles.

Barriers to change: case study B

Marcie, the deputy manager of a full daycare setting, has been informed by senior line managers that the team will be expected to expand their current work to include a new project. The team have come to expect these regular requests but their experience is that the senior team soon forget a project once another is on the horizon – they see it merely as jumping onto the latest bandwagon.

At the team meeting, Marcie explains the new project and asks for two volunteers to attend a conference to learn more about the project and how it will be monitored and evaluated. Tomas looks at Marcie and exclaims: 'Oh, not again, why can't we just concentrate on one thing at a time? Why is it always us that have to take on new initiatives? What about Clarissa's team? They never take on anything new…. And, as for going to the conference: well that means a 6am train. You don't see any of Clarissa's team getting up at 5am to catch a train.' Marcie is about to answer when Selma leans forward and says: 'I know what you mean Tomas, all this change: it can't be good for us. Why can't we just leave things as they are? Don't fix it if it's not broken, that's my motto.'

Questions:

- How as a leader might you handle the situation in case study B?

- If the response of the team B staff was a typical one, one that Marcie might have anticipated, how might she have handled it differently?

- If the response was unusual and unexpected, what course of action would you take if you were Marcie?

Approaching change together

When practitioners have had the opportunity for their point of view to be listened to and have taken part in dialogue about the advantages and disadvantages of possible courses of action, the leader needs to facilitate team commitment on the way forward. For a strong possibility of good outcomes, the team needs to work effectively together. Being clear about this team approach means that there is much less likelihood of a member sabotaging the improvement effort.

A good leader will also recognise and praise the efforts made by those who were against the actions that were decided. For example, when suggesting a continuous snack routine, there may be practitioners who say, having tried it before, that it will not work. One of the many ways in which the leader could support the change would be by thanking the doubting practitioner for 'having a go' and praising the effort as well as the achievements made towards the team goal.

In addition to embracing change, engaging with CQI means being prepared to make choices, take risks and potentially make mistakes.

Taking risks in a secure environment to enable change and innovation

As it states in the EYFS practice guidance (p. 27) … children … make choices that involve challenge, when adults ensure their safety … show increasing confidence in new situations … what they need is our support to do it in a safe and secure environment.

(Garvey 2007, p. 9)

This also applies to the teams with whom we work. We want teams and practitioners who make choices and show increasing confidence in new situations. The role of the Leader as a Developer is to offer support to enable this to happen in a safe and secure environment without fear of recrimination or ridicule by leaders or peers. This is not to suggest that you throw all caution to the wind. For example, moving the furniture to try out a new idea, or discovering that it is not helpful to have the book area next to the music area, is not going to cause any real damage and can easily be rectified.

Taking risks is not about reckless change. In this context, taking risks is about trying out new ideas and having a go. For leaders it might be delegating some responsibility to a new member of staff or it could be, for example, letting someone else do the newsletter or greet the parents. Practitioners may need support with these new tasks at first and you may be tempted to think that it is quicker and easier to do it yourself, but in the long run it is about supporting staff to develop their skills and knowledge and is a way of ensuring continuous quality improvement (see Chapter 3 on making mistakes, risk and challenge).

Planned and unplanned change

As well as change that we plan for and try to implement, there is change that is unplanned. For example, a key member of staff resigns, there is a major flood and you have to move buildings for a length of time, a new provider opens in the next street and you wonder if this will affect your business, a provider closes in the next street and you cannot keep up with the demand for places, etc. Unplanned change can lead to crisis management or be reactive. It can pose threats and offer opportunities. Leaders need to be able to navigate through these experiences and spot the opportunities when they occur.

Sometimes change is an organic process; you do not plan for it to happen but by trial and error or happenchance changes take place that work well and stick. Where leaders create a culture of risk taking and creativity, such change is more likely to occur.

The following reflection looks at a situation where change is intended to be a positive experience, but does not go quite according to plan.

Reflection: case study

Unexpected outcomes

Freya, the manager and owner of a large nursery, is well liked in the nursery and has a staff team who are committed to the children and families, and to the nursery. Freya knows her staff team are dedicated and is always looking for ways to show her appreciation.

Freya notices a training course on 'motivation, praise and encouragement' and immediately books a place. Freya returns to the nursery and is buzzing with enthusiasm and excitement, and cannot wait to try out some of the ideas from the training course. In order to reward her dedicated team Freya uses one of the suggestions from the training course and sets up a 'team awards' process. There is an award for 'team member of the month', 'colleague of the month' and a 'new ideas award'. Freya asks team members to vote for each other in each category and announces that the person with the most votes will win the award in that category. After two weeks Freya goes to empty the voting box and is surprised to find only a handful of votes.

At the team meeting Freya mentions the 'team awards' and queries why there are so few votes. The team look uncomfortable for a while, but eventually someone says, 'Well, actually Freya, we don't like them'. Freya is taken aback by this and asks for further comments. After a while it becomes apparent that the team feel the awards are artificial. The team agree that they all feel valued by Freya, and that they regularly receive thanks and praise that is warm, honest and timely but that the 'team awards' feel contrived and appear to almost encourage the team to be in competition with each other.

Questions:

Can you think of any occasions in your personal or work life where things did not go according to plan or the outcome was different to your expectation?

Have you any idea why this was?

In hindsight, do you think you could have managed the situation more appropriately to achieve a different outcome?

Sometimes we use strategies that have worked for us before or, as in Freya's case, we borrow strategies that have worked for someone else in a different context (think about how we learn parenting skills).

The difference between your context and the context from which you have borrowed may be marked or subtle, many or few, and the difference in outcome could be negligible or huge. Each context presents its own complexities that a leader may or may not be able to read and navigate.

> *Leadership in early years is a complex concept and its role in quality provision has not been well understood by many of those who work in the early years field to date.*

> (Rodd 2005, p. 2)

Measuring quality: international perspectives

The importance of leadership and management in bringing about quality improvement and good outcomes for children and families has been identified globally. Countries as diverse as Chile, Australia and the UK are undergoing reform in terms of the early years and playwork sector. This global development and the increased use of the internet as a way of sharing information can be of great benefit to the Leader as a Developer. There are lessons to be learnt, comparisons to be made and advice to take note of.

In 2008, the Journal of Early Childhood Matters published a special edition on quality. In it they considered measuring quality in a range of different countries. Peralta, who was based in Chile, researched the literature surrounding quality in the early years and came up with the following:

> *Analysis of the quality criteria highlighted by research shows the most influential factors in childhood education in order of their impact are as follows:*
>
> - *the contribution of parents*
>
> - *the quality of interaction*
>
> - *an explicit, clear and relevant educational programme*
>
> - *monitoring and evaluation systems*

- *adequate and organised physical spaces*

- *stable routines*

- *ongoing training and preparation for the work team*

- *children taking an active role in their own learning*

(Peralta 2008, p. 7)

In Australia, the National Childcare Accreditation Council (NCAC) is funded by the Department of Education, Employment and Workplace Relations (DEEWR) to administer Child Care Quality Assurance (CCQA). The Council of Australian Governments (COAG) consulted in September 2008 on 'A National Framework for Early Childhood Education and Care'. NCAC have offered the following 'key drivers of quality'.

The key drivers of quality included in the standards should focus on quality outcomes for children and should include:

- *staffing requirements and arrangements (ratios, qualifications, group sizes)*

- *leadership and management*

- *relationships between staff and children*

- *family and community partners*

- *differentiated play-based curriculum*

- *physical environment (both in terms of structure and facilities, but also as the 'third teacher')*

- *health, hygiene and safety*

- *child protection*

- *professional knowledge and continuing professional development for educators.*

The standards must recognise that children's needs change over time and they [the standards] should reflect children of all ages and in a variety of childcare settings.

(www.ncac.gov.au)

Many of the key drivers outlined above have been incorporated into *Belonging, Being and Becoming: The Early Years Learning Framework for Australia* (2009) which in turn will be incorporated into the National Quality Standards, and will include drivers such as ratios and qualifications, etc.

In England, the NQIN have produced *The Companion Guide to the Quality Improvement Principles* (2008) which offers five themes for quality improvement:

1. Improvement of outcomes in early years and childcare settings
2. Inclusive values and principles that address inequalities
3. Continuous self-evaluation and reflective practice
4. Effective leadership and workforce planning
5. Effective monitoring and evaluation of practice and outcomes

Leadership and ongoing training play a key part in the global view of quality, and there is much to be learnt from global work on developing quality. However, the Leader as a Developer is aware that an idea cannot simply be transposed from one country to, say, deepest Yorkshire or Inner-city London. The challenge of CQI for the leader is to take the learning and make it appropriate to the children, young people, families and communities in their village, town or city.

Chapter summary

Strong leadership is a key indicator of ability to 'Narrow the Gap' between the most vulnerable children and the rest, leading to improved outcomes for all. This is an important function of quality improvement. This chapter introduces terminology used to describe quality and approaches to quality improvement.

In order to improve quality, leaders need to be able to not only lead self-evaluation processes for their organisation but also implement the required changes. They need to encourage others to share in the responsibility for identifying and implementing these improvements.

Continuous professional development can take place in many ways, including learning from experience and sharing practice.

As well as looking at the quality of service provided, it is also important to consider outcomes and see whether the changes made have made a difference to the key stakeholders.

The chapter introduces Outcomes Based Accountability (OBA), as well as the theory of change management, including attitudes, resistance and barriers to change and also approaches for action planning and involving the whole team.

Endnote: Reflecting on Leadership

Becoming a leader for quality is to embark on a journey for which there is no defined destination. There will always be something new to learn, different way of doing things and new challenges. The most effective leaders are learners, enablers, mentors, champions, motivators, problem solvers and developers. Leaders encourage these attributes in others in order to develop their leadership skills and share the responsibility for improving quality. Effective leaders are mindful of the importance of supportive and nurturing relationships, where individuals, teams and communities are enabled to come together to debate, challenge, take risks and find solutions in order to raise quality.

New research, knowledge, reflection and experiences will influence thinking and practice, and will impact on understanding of quality. As we learn more about quality, so are we likely to learn more about the influence that leaders and managers have on the quality of experience offered to children and families. You are an important researcher in the quest to understand leadership for quality. As you develop your knowledge and your experiences, so this will add to the shared understanding of what works in terms of leadership in the early years and playwork sectors. Leading for quality and making a difference for all children should make your job among the most rewarding leadership roles available.

At times your role may seem challenging and complex. Reflection, feedback, self-evaluation, challenge, change, debate and dialogue should be used as ways of developing effective practice and every situation seen as a learning opportunity. As you learn more about your leadership, this book will encourage and empower you to use your mentoring, enabling and motivational skills, to problem solve along the way and champion the things you believe in.

There will be periods of calm and periods of chaos during your leadership role, whatever the level. Think of the periods of stability in your work background: everything going smoothly, quality at a high level and everyone committed to their part within the organisation. Then the manager leaves, or several staff are suddenly ill – chaos ensues and perhaps there is a wobble in the quality of provision offered. Some people cope admirably with a period of chaos, others do not. This is where leadership skills can be tested to the limit. You will need to lead your team through the challenge and chaos – it may help to think of this as a journey.

Your team set out on a voyage of discovery – you are at the helm of the ship, ready to lead this intrepid group of practitioners. You set out from a point in time. You cross many waters and see many places to land: some are rocky, others calm and blue with sandy beaches, where you and your team can rest awhile. Some offer new vistas not considered before. As you travel there may well be thunderstorms and you may need support in order to steer. Of all the lands you visit, some will be more appealing than others. Some will offer respite and some challenge. At some places you will want to stay for a while and others you will be glad to leave. All will have an influence on you and your team in some way.

After adventuring in these lands it will be time to re-organise for the rest of the journey. Your team may well have changed. Some will have moved on and others will have joined. You may need time to repair after storms, to re-allocate roles, some things will need updating and new ideas that you picked up will need consideration.

This book has been a tour of leadership. It is one map of some of the places you could explore. Leadership is a personal adventure made up of a range of journeys of discovery, and the ideas outlined here are just some of those that may help.

We would like the final word to go to Mark Twain, who said:

> *Twenty years from now you will be more disappointed by the things that you did not do than by the ones you did do. So throw off the bowlines. Sail away from the safe harbour. Catch the trade winds in your sails. Explore. Dream. Discover.*

> (Mark Twain)

Bibliography

Preface

Department for Children, Schools and Families (2008) *Raising Standards – Improving Outcomes Statutory Guidance: Early Years Outcomes Duty Childcare Act 2006*. Nottingham: DCSF.

Department for Education and Skills (2004) *Choice for Parents, the Best Start for Children: A Ten-Year Strategy for Childcare*. Nottingham: DfES.

Fullan, M (2007) *The New Meaning of Educational Change*. 4th ed. New York: Teachers College Press.

Martin, K, Lord, P, White, R and Atkinson, M (2009) *Narrowing the Gap in Outcomes: Leadership* (LGA Research Report). Slough: NFER.

Munton, Anthony G and Mooney, Ann (2001) *Integrating Self-Assessment into Statutory Inspection Procedures: The Impact on the Quality of Group Day Care Provision*. Nottingham: DfES.

Ofsted (2008) *Early Years: Leading to Excellence*. London: Ofsted. Available at http://www.ofsted.gov.uk/Ofsted-home/Leading-to-excellence

Ofsted (2009) *Early Years Self-Evaluation Form Guidance*. Last accessed September 2009 at http://www.ofsted.gov.uk/Ofsted-home/Forms-and-guidance/Browse-all-by/Other/General/Early-years-online-self-evaluation-form-SEF-and-guidance-For-settings-delivering-the-Early-Years-Foundation-Stage/(language)/eng-GB

Rodd, J (2006) *Leadership in Early Childhood: The Pathway to Professionalism*. 3rd ed. Maidenhead: Open University Press.

Siraj-Blatchford, I and Manni, L (2007) *Effective Leadership in the Early Years Sector: The ELEYS Study*. London: Institute of Education.

Introduction

Bass, B and Stodgill, R (1990) *Bass and Stodgill's Handbook of Leadership: Theory, Research, and Managerial Applications*. 3rd ed. New York: Free Press.

Bennis, W and Nanus, B (1977) *Leaders: Strategies for Taking Charge*. Cambridge, MA: Harvard Business Review Press.

Blake, R and Mouton, J (1964) *The Managerial Grid: The Key to Leadership Excellence*. Houston, TX: Gulf.

Gregoire, MB and Arendt, SW (2004) 'Leadership: Reflections over the Last 100 years', *Journal of the American Dietetic Association*, 104, 395–403.

Jones, C and Pound, L (2008) *Leadership and Management in the Early Years: A Practical Guide*. Maidenhead: Open University Press.

Kellerman, B and Webster, S (2001) 'The Recent Literature on Public Leadership Reviewed and Considered', *The Leadership Quarterly*, 12 (4), 485–514.

Kotter, J (1999) *What Leaders Really Do*. Cambridge, MA: Harvard Business School Press.

Murray, M (1975) 'Comparing Public and Private Management: An Exploratory Essay', *Public Administration Review*, 35, 364–371.

Rodd, J (2006) *Leadership in Early Childhood: The Pathway to Professionalism*. 3rd ed. Maidenhead: Open University Press.

Scrivens, C (2002) 'Constructions of Leadership: Does Gender Make a Difference? – Perspectives from an English Speaking Country', in Nivala, V and Hujala, E (eds) *Leadership in Early Childhood Education: Cross-Cultural Perspectives*. Department of Educational Sciences and Teacher Education: University of Oulu.

Simkins, T (2005) 'Leadership in Education "What Works" or "What Makes Sense?"', *Educational Management Administration and Leadership*, 33 (1), 9–26.

Siraj-Blatchford, I and Manni, L (2007) *Effective Leadership in the Early Years Sector: The ELEYS Study*. London: Institute of Education. Last accessed October 2008 at http://www.gtce.org.uk/shared/contentlibs/126795/93128/120213/eleys_study.pdf

Tannenbaum, R and Schmidt, W (1958) 'How to Choose a Leadership Pattern', *Harvard Business Review*, 36 (2), 95–101.

West-Burnham, J (2004) *Building Leadership Capacity – Helping Leaders Learn: An NCSL Think Piece*. Nottingham: National College for School Leadership.

Wood, J and Wood, M (2000) *Frederick Winslow Taylor*. Abingdon: Routledge.

Zaleznik, A (1977) 'Managers and Leaders: Are They Different?', *Harvard Business Review*, 55 (3), 67–78.

1 Developing your Leadership

Gleick, J (1987) *Chaos: Making a New Science*. London: Vintage.

Goleman, D, Boyatzis, R and McKee, A (2002) *The New Leaders: Transforming the Art of Leadership into the Science of Results*. London: Sphere.

Mintzberg, H (2004) *Managers Not MBAs*. London: FT Prentice-Hall.

Morgan, G (1997) *Images of Organization*. 2nd ed. Thousand Oaks, CA: Sage.

Moyles, J (2006) *Effective Leadership and Management in the Early Years*. London: Open University Press.

Northouse, P (2007) *Leadership: Theory and Practice*. London: Sage.

Wheatley, M (1999) *Leadership and the New Science: Discovering Order in a Chaotic World*. San Francisco: Berrett-Koehler.

2 The Leader as a Learner

Bolton, G (2001) *Reflective Practice: Writing and Professional Development*. London: Paul Chapman.

Dewey, J (1953) *How We Think*. Boston, D.C. Heath and Co.

Dunn, K and Dunn, R (1998) *Complete Guide to Learning Style In-Service Systems*. Switzerland: Allyn & Bacon.

Gibbs, G (1988) *Learning by Doing: A Guide to Teaching and Learning Methods*. Oxford: Further Educational Unit, Oxford Polytechnic.

Gregorc, AF (1985) *Inside Styles: Beyond the Basics*. Maynard, MA: Gabriel Systems.

Honey, P and Mumford, A (1986) *The Manual of Learning Styles*. Maidenhead: Peter Honey.

Johns C (2000) *Becoming a Reflective Practitioner: a Reflective and Holistic Approach to Clinical Nursing, Practice Development and Clinical Supervision*. Oxford: Blackwell Science.

Kolb, DA and Fry, R (1975) 'Toward an Applied Theory of Experiential Learning', in Cooper, C (ed) *Theories of Group Process*. London: John Wiley.

Moon, J (1999) *Reflection in Learning and Professional Development*. London: Kogan Page.

Moon, J (2004) *A Handbook on Reflective and Experiential Learning: Theory and Practice*. 2nd ed. Oxon: RoutledgeFalmer.

Moon, J (2005) *Learning Journals: A Handbook for Reflective Practice and Professional Development.* 2nd ed. London: Routledge.

Rolfe, G, Freshwater, D and Jasper, M (2001) *Critical Reflection in Nursing and the Helping Professions: a User's Guide.* Basingstoke: Palgrave Macmillan.

3 The Leader as an Enabler

Adair, J (1998) *Effective Leadership.* London: Pan Books.

Behar, H (2007) *It's Not About the Coffee.* New York: Penguin/Portfolio.

Crosby, PB (1984) *Quality Without Tears: The Art of Hassle-Free Management.* New York: McGraw Hill.

de Bono, E (1985) *Six Thinking Hats.* Boston: Little Brown and Company http://www.edwdebono.com [first accessed May 2008].

Greenleaf, RK (1977) *Servant Leadership. A Journey into the Nature of Legitimate Power and Greatness.* New Jersey: Paulist Press.

http://www.greenleaf.org [last accessed September 2009].

http://www.kindengezin.be [last accessed September 2009].

Laevers, F, Daems, M, De Bruyckere, G, Declercq, B, Moons, J, Silkens, K, Snoeck G and van Kessel, M (2005) *SICS (Well Being and Involvement) Manual.* Flanders: Research Centre for Experiential Education, Leuven University.

4 The Leader as a Mentor

http://www.bobgriffiths.com [last accessed September 2009].

http://www.coachingnetwork.org.uk [last accessed September 2009].

Department for Education and Skills (2007) *The Early Years Foundation Stage: Setting the Standards for Learning, Development and Care for Children from Birth to Five.* Nottingham: DfES.

Griffiths, B and Kaday, C (2004) *GROW Your Own Carrot.* London: Hodder Headline.

Johnson, WB and Ridley, CR (2004) *The Elements of Mentoring.* New York: Palgrave Macmillan.

Shea, GF (1992) *Mentoring: A Guide to the Basics.* California: Crisp.

Whitmore, J (2002). *Coaching For Performance: Growing People, Performance and Purpose.* 3rd ed. London: Nicholas Brealey.

5 The Leader as a Champion

Children's Workforce Development Council (2007) *Guidance to the Standards for the Award of Early Years Professional Status*. Leeds: CWDC.

Cooper, G, Goldsack, C, Pace, C and Williams, P (2007) *Quality Improvement Principles: A Framework for Local Authorities and National Organisations to Improve Quality Outcomes for Children and Young People*. London: NCB.

Covey, SR (1992) *The 7 Habits of Highly Effective People: Powerful Lessons in Personal Change*. First published 1989. London: Simon & Schuster.

Cuno, J (2005) 'Telling Stories: Rhetoric and Leadership, a Case Study', *Leadership*, (1), 205–213.

Friedman, Mark (2005) *Trying Hard Is Not Good Enough: How to Produce Measurable Improvements for Customers and Communities*. Victoria, BC: Trafford.

Gladwell, M (2000) *The Tipping Point: How Little Things Can Make a Big Difference*. London: Little Brown.

HM Government (2008) *Raising Standards – Improving Outcomes Statutory Guidance: Early Years Outcomes Duty Childcare Act 2006*. Nottingham: DCSF.

Martin, K, Lord, P, White, R and Atkinson, M (2009) *Narrowing the Gap in Outcomes: Leadership* (LGA Research Report). Slough: NFER.

Mintzberg, H (1999) 'Managing Quietly', *Leader to Leader*, (Spring),12.

Ofsted (2009) *Early Years Self-Evaluation Form Guidance*. Last accessed September 2009 at http://www.ofsted.gov.uk/Ofsted-home/Forms-and-guidance/Browse-all-by/Other/General/Early-years-online-self-evaluation-form-SEF-and-guidance-For-settings-delivering-the-Early-Years-Foundation-Stage/(language)/eng-GB

Senge, P (2006) *The Fifth Discipline: The Art and Practice of The Learning Organisation*. Rev. ed. London: Random House.

Senge, P, Scharmer, CO, Jaworski, J and Flowers, B (2005) *Presence: Exploring Profound Change in People, Organizations and Society*. London: Nicholas Brealey.

Siraj-Blatchford, I and Manni, L (2007) *Effective Leadership in the Early Years Sector: The ELEYS Study*. London: Institute of Education.

Torres, RM (2008) 'Looking After Society's Treasures: The Challenge of Early Childhood', *Journal of Early Childhood Matters*, (110) 3, 13–18.

6 The Leader as a Motivator

Gagné, RM (1985) *The Conditions of Learning*. New York: Holt, Rinehart and Winston.

Gleick, J (1987) *Chaos: Making a New Science*. London: Vintage.

Maslow, A (1970) *Motivation and Personality*. 2nd ed. New York: Harper and Row.

Moon, J (1999) *Reflection in Learning and Professional Development*. London: Kogan Page.

Vygotsky, LS (1978) *Mind in Society: Development of Higher Psychological Processes*. Cambridge, MA: Harvard University Press.

7 The Leader as a Problem Solver

Ancona, D, Malone, TW, Orlikowski, W J and Senge, P (2007) 'In Praise of the Incomplete Leader', *Harvard Business Review*, Feb 2007, 92–100.

Department for Children, Schools and Families (2008) *EYQISP: Early Years Quality Improvement Support Programme*. Nottingham: DCSF.

Department for Education and Skills (2007) *The Early Years Foundation Stage: Setting the Standards for Learning, Development and Care for Children from Birth to Five*. Nottingham: DfES.

Friedman, Mark (2005) *Trying Hard Is Not Good Enough: How to Produce Measurable Improvements for Customers and Communities*. Victoria, BC: Trafford.

Moullin, M (2002) *Delivering Excellence in Health and Social Care*. Buckingham: Open University Press.

Oakland, J (2003) *Total Quality Management: Text with Cases*. 3rd ed. Oxford: Elsevier Butterworth–Heinemann.

Pyzdek, T (2003) *The Six Sigma Handbook*. Rev. and expanded. New York: McGraw-Hill.

Schön, DA (1983) *The Reflective Practitioner: How Professionals Think in Action*. Aldershot: Ashgate.

Tarbitt, V (2005) *Module 1& 2: Mentoring*. Leeds: Leeds Metropolitan University.

Tuckman, Bruce W (1965) 'Developmental Sequence in Small Groups', *Psychological Bulletin*, 63, 384–399. The article was reprinted in *Group Facilitation: A Research and Applications Journal*, 3, Spring 2001 and is available as a Word document: http://dennislearningcenter.osu.edu/

references/GROUP%20DEV%20ARTICLE.doc accessed January 14, 2005. Source http://www.infed.org/thinkers/tuckman.htm [last accessed September 2009].

Tuckman, Bruce W and Jensen, Mary Ann C (1977) 'Stages of Small Group Development Revisited', *Group and Organizational Studies*, 2, 419–427.

8 The Leader as a Developer

Black, P and Wiliam, D (2001) *Inside the Black Box: Raising Standards Through Classroom Assessment*. London: King's College, School of Education.

Covey, SR (1992) *The 7 Habits of Highly Effective People: Powerful Lessons in Personal Change*. First published 1989. London: Simon & Schuster.

Crosby, Philip B (1979) *Quality is Free: The Art of Making Quality Certain*. New York: McGraw-Hill.

http://www.deewr.gov.au/EarlyChildhood/Policy_Agenda/Quality/Pages/EarlyYearsLearningFramework.aspx [last accessed September 2009].

Deming, W Edwards (1982) *Out of the Crisis*. Cambridge, MA: MIT Press.

Department for Children, Schools and Families (2007) *The Children's Plan: Building Brighter Futures*. Nottingham: DCSF.

Department for Children, Schools and Families (2008a) *EYQISP: Early Years Quality Improvement Support Programme*. Nottingham: DCSF.

Department for Children, Schools and Families (2008b) *Better Outcomes for Children and Young People: From Talk to Action*. Nottingham: DCSF. Last accessed September 2009 at http://www.dcsf.gov.uk/everychildmatters/resources-and-practice/IG00327/

Department for Children, Schools and Families (2009a) *Progress Matters: Reviewing and Enhancing Young Children's Development*. Nottingham: DCSF.

Department for Children, Schools and Families (2009b) *Your Child's Early Learning and Care: Birth to Five – Ideas and Support for You*. Nottingham: DCSF.

Department for Education and Skills (2007) *The Early Years Foundation Stage: Setting the Standards for Learning, Development and Care for Children from Birth to Five*. Nottingham: DfES.

Friedman, Mark (2005) *Trying Hard Is Not Good Enough: How to Produce Measurable Improvements for Customers and Communities*. Victoria, BC: Trafford.

Fullan, M (2007) *The New Meaning of Educational Change.* 4th ed. New York: Teachers College Press.

Garvey, D (2007) *Practical Pre-school Magazine: Balancing Risk and Challenge.* Issue 79. London: Step Forward.

Garvin, DA (1984) 'What does Product Quality Really Mean?', *Sloan Management Review*, 26, 25–43.

Gladwell, M (2000) *The Tipping Point: How Little Things Can Make a Big Difference.* London: Little Brown.

Gopnik, Alison, Meltzoff, Andrew N and Kohl, Patricia K (1999) *How Babies Think: The Science of Childhood.* London: Phoenix.

Investors in People at http://www.investorsinpeople.co.uk [last accessed September 2009].

Juran, JM (1989) *Juran on Leadership for Quality: An Executive Handbook.* New York: Free Press.

Martin, K, Lord, P, White, R and Atkinson, M (2009) *Narrowing the Gap in Outcomes: Leadership* (LGA Research Report). Slough: NFER.

Munton, AG and Mooney, A (2001) *Integrating Self-Assessment into Statutory Inspection Procedures: The Impact on the Quality of Group Day Care Provision.* Nottingham: DfES.

http://www.ncac.gov.au/ [last accessed September 2009].

Oakland, J (2003) *Total Quality Management: Text with Cases.* 3rd ed. Oxford: Elsevier Butterworth–Heinemann.

Ofsted (2008) *Early Years: Leading to Excellence.* London: Ofsted. Last accessed September 2009 at http://www.ofsted.gov.uk/Ofsted-home/ Leading-to-excellence

Ofsted (2009) *Early Years Self-Evaluation Form Guidance.* Last accessed September 2009 at http://www.ofsted.gov.uk/Ofsted-home/Forms-and-guidance/Browse-all-by/Other/General/Early-years-online-self-evaluation-form-SEF-and-guidance-For-settings-delivering-the-Early-Years-Foundation-Stage/(language)/eng-GB

Peralta, MV (2008) 'Quality: Children's Right to Appropriate and Relevant Education,' *Journal of Early Childhood Matters*, (110) 3, 3–12.

Rodd, J (2005) 'Leadership: An Essential Ingredient or an Optional Extra for Quality Early Childhood Provision?' A Discussion Paper. http://www.tactyc.org.uk/pdfs/rodd.pdf

Senge, P (2006) *The Fifth Discipline: The Art and Practice of the Learning Organisation.* Rev. ed. London: Random House.

Senge, P, Scharmer, CO, Jaworski, J and Flowers, BS (2005) *Presence: Exploring Profound Change in People, Organizations and Society*. London: Nicholas Brearley.

Stepien, D, Alwyine-Mosely, J, Finch, S and Garvey, D (2008) *The NQIN Companion Guide to the Quality Improvement Principles: A Framework for Local Authorities and National Organisations to Improve Quality Outcomes for Children and Young People*. London: NCB.

Stoll, L and Fink, D (1996) *Changing Our Schools: Linking School Effectiveness and School Improvement*. Buckingham: Open University Press.

Sylva, K, Sammons, P, Melhuish, E, Siraj-Blatchford, I, Taggart, B, Hunt, S and Jelicic, H (2008) *Effective Pre-School and Primary Education 3-11 Project (EPPE 3-11): Influences on Children's Cognitive and Social Development in Year 6*. Nottingham: DCSF. Last accessed September 2009 at http://publications.dcsf.gov.uk/eOrderingDownload/DCSF-RB048-049.pdf

Useful websites

Early Years Education, Childcare and Playwork Websites

http://www.continyou.org.uk/

http://www.continyou.org.uk/what_we_do/children_and_young_people/breakfast_club_plus

http://www.c4eo.org.uk/

http://www.cwdcouncil.org.uk/

http://www.daycaretrust.org.uk/

http://www.dcsf.gov.uk/index.htm

http://www.everychildmatters.gov.uk/

http://www.4children.org.uk/

http://www.infed.org/lifelonglearning/b-andra.htm

http://www.londonplay.org.uk/

http://www.kids.org.uk/

http://www.ncb.org.uk/

http://www.ncb.org.uk/qualityimprovement

http://www.nurseryworld.co.uk/

http://www.ofsted.gov.uk/

http://www.playengland.org.uk/

http://www.playwales.org.uk/

http://www.playscotland.org/

http://www.peal.org.uk/

http://www.practicalpreschool.com/

http://www.skillsactive.com/playwork

http://www.skillsactive.com/playwork/principles

http://www.surestart.gov.uk/

http://www.standards.dcsf.gov.uk/eyfs/

http://www.tactyc.org.uk/default.asp

http://www.tda.gov.uk/

http://www.teachernet.gov.uk/

http://www.teachingexpertise.com/

http://www.timeshighereducation.co.uk/

http://www.trainingjournal.com/index.php

Leadership/management websites

http://www.businessballs.com/leadership.htm

http://www.businesslink.gov.uk/

http://www.cwdcouncil.org.uk/eyps

http://www.coachingnetwork.org.uk/Default.htm

http://www.improvementfoundation.org/

http://www.johnadair.co.uk/index.html

http://www.maslow.com/

http://www.mindtools.com/

http://www.nationalcollege.org.uk/

http://www.peterhoney.com/

http://www.raguide.org/

http://www.resultsaccountability.com/

http://www.teachernet.gov.uk/management/

http://www.teachingexpertise.com/leadership-management

Index